DATE DUE

APR 1 8 1978		

DEMCO 38-297

D1280929

The Folklore of the British Isles
General Editor: Venetia J. Newall

The Folklore
of Somerset

Other books in the present series:

General Editor: Venetia J. Newall

Jacqueline Simpson *The Folklore of Sussex* (1973)
Enid Porter *The Folklore of East Anglia* (1974)
Sean O'Sullivan *The Folklore of Ireland* (1974)
Katherine Briggs *The Folklore of the Cotswolds* (1974)
Ernest Marwick *The Folklore of Orkney & Shetland* (1975)
Tony Deane & Tony Shaw *The Folklore of Cornwall* (1975)
Margaret Killip *The Folklore of the Isle of Man* (1976)
Ralph Whitlock *The Folklore of Wiltshire* (1976)
Wendy Boase *The Folklore of Hampshire & Isle of Wight* (1976)
Roy Palmer *The Folklore of Warwickshire* (1976)
Anne Ross *The Folklore of the Highlands* (1976)
Jacqueline Simpson *The Folklore of the Welsh Border* (1976)
Marjorie Rowling *The Folklore of the Lake District* (1976)

The Folklore
of Somerset

KINGSLEY PALMER

Drawings by Gay John Galsworthy

ROWMAN AND LITTLEFIELD
Totowa, New Jersey

To Freyd

First published in the United States 1976
by Rowman and Littlefield, Totowa, N.J.

© Kingsley Palmer, 1976

ISBN 0-87471-807-4

Printed in Great Britain

Contents

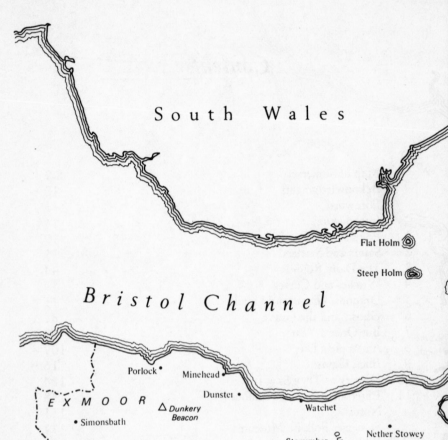

South Wales

Bristol Channel

Flat Holm

Steep Holm

Porlock • Minehead •

Dunster •

EXMOOR △ Dunkery
Beacon

Watchet

• Simonsbath

Nether Stowey

Stogumber •

Bridgwater

• Withypool

BRENDON HILLS

Crowcombe •

QUANTOCK HILLS

Tarr Steps

Bishop's
Lydeard •

N

• Dulverton

Wiveliscombe •

Norton
Fitzwarren •

Taunton

TAUNTON VALE

Hatch
Beauchamp

• Wellington

Staple Fitzpaine •

Culmstock
•

Churchstanton •

Bishop's Wood •

Buckland •
St Mary

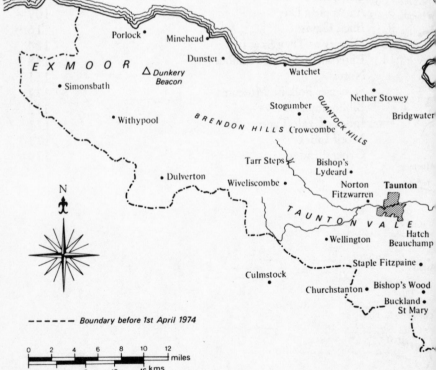

– – – – – Boundary before 1st April 1974

0   2   4   6   8   10   12
miles
4   8   12   16 kms

SOMERSET

MOUTH OF THE SEVERN

Portishead

Clevedon • Nailsea • Bristol

DUNDRY HILL

Keynsham

Weston-Super-Mare • Congresbury

Chew Stoke • Stanton Drew
Chew Magna Bath

Chew Valley Lake

Freshford

Farleigh Hungerford

MENDIP HILLS

Axbridge • Cheddar

Radstock

Midsomer Norton

△ Brent Knoll

Burnham-on-Sea

Chewton Mendip

Priddy

Mells • Frome

Highbridge • Wedmore • Wookey Hole

Brue

Wells •

Meare •

Shepton Mallet

Chedzoy POLDEN HILLS

△ TOR
Glastonbury

Evercreech

SELWOOD

✕ Sedgemoor

Bruton •

Athelney

Tone

Somerton

Castle Cary •

Wincanton •

Parret

Langport

Muchelney • Yeo

◇ Cadbury Castle

Curry • Mallet • Hambridge

Ilchester

Milborne Port

Templecombe

Martock
Montacute

Barrington

Ashill

South △ HAM HILL
Petherton

Yeovil

• Ilminster

Dowlish Wake •

Combe St Nicholas

• Chard

Hinton St George

WINDWHISTLE HILLS

• Crewkerne

Acknowledgments

I wish to thank the following authors and publishers for permission to quote from the following books and journals (page numbers refer to *The Folklore of Somerset*):

Chard and Ilminster News (Nov. 1973), p. 106.

Coleman, D. N. 'Cider Making in North and Central Somerset', Leeds University BA thesis, p. 149.

Hurley, J. *Legends of Exmoor* (Williton, 1973), pp. 22-23, 27, 66 and 131.

Mee, A. *The King's England* (Somerset), pp. 125 and 128.

Tongue, R. L. & Briggs, K. M. (ed) *Somerset Folklore* (Folklore Society, 1965), p. 51.

Wyatt, I. *The Book of Huish* (Western Gazette Co. Ltd, Yeovil, c. 1933), pp. 93 and 133.

Foreword

'Milk rendered immortal' is surely the perfect description of cheese. Cheddar, renowned and imitated throughout the world, is Somerset's memorial to the ingenuity of the dairymaid. Locally it is regarded as therapeutic – to ensure that they will bear children, the girls in a household used to share out the first slice of a groaning cheese.

Somerset cheese is said to have been a chance invention. A forgetful milkmaid left her pail in a cave up the Gorge. Time passed, and, when she remembered to collect it, the milk had turned into Cheddar. The variety as such is first mentioned in 1600 and, since the caves are quite unsuited to cheese production, the tradition is fantasy – like Camden's statement, that dairying skills arrived with the Romans. Societies that keep livestock usually evolve straightforward cheese-making methods, and the Veneti, quite a sophisticated community, were in the Mendips when Caesar first reached Britain.

A century later, the Roman invaders had established the Mendip lead mines. They colonised an area where the Dumnonii and the Belgae had already overcome the Veneti, probably substituting a hilltop border for the earlier Wansdyke boundary. A great marsh – almost an inland sea – separated the Mendips from the southerly hills. Thus, by attaching north Somerset (now in Avon) to the Wiltshire 'Canton of the Belgae,' Roman administration reflected the tribal and geographical situation.

Glastonbury, once a flourishing Venetic settlement, was then an island, apparently one of seven. Dumnonia (Devon) regained it when the Romans withdrew, extending its frontiers almost to the present Somerset-Avon border. One interesting legend of a reputed ancient Lordship of Avon survives. Vincent, its Belgic ruler, fought against the giant, Gorm; rocks and promontories north of Bridgwater Bay are the giant's bones, marking the spot where he tripped and fell. Vincent's chair is at Blaise Castle, near Bristol, now a folk museum.

When the Saxons arrived, Glastonbury was still in Dumnonia. In the mid-seventh century they annexed this watery area, but the Celtic monastery, which had long been a famous shrine, survived, with its new Saxon counterpart. Circumstantial and traditional arguments suggest that it may perhaps represent Christianity's first foothold in Britain; the link with Arthur, whether real or legendary, stresses the importance of the site.

In those days many courtly pilgrims came to the west country. Later the Mendips were to provide a hunting ground for the Wessex kings. Many of their successors favoured Exmoor, and it remained a Royal Forest until the end of George III's reign. Today it is still the home of wild red deer, though Somerset is chiefly famed for its orchards. Few people are aware that cider was once a king's drink. It was provided in the mid-eleventh century, at Harold Godwinson's banqueting table in the west country, before he became king. The record is from Hereford, but the drink must have been known in Somerset at the same period. In the following century William of Malmesbury describes the monks of Glastonbury on feast days, with 'mead in their cans and wine in their grace-cup' – which was probably apple wine. They are not known to have planted vines before the thirteenth century.

Wassailing the apple trees was once a widespread Somerset custom. The word is Germanic and corresponds, if tradition is correct, to the first known greeting of the fifth-century continental intruders. In about 450, Hengist, a Frisian or Jutish adventurer, ingratiated himself with Vortigern, British ruler of Kent and the south-east. To ensnare the Briton, he presented his beautiful daughter, Hrothwina. She greeted the King, addressed him *Wacht Heil,* and offered a cup of wine – presumably cider. Soon after, Vortigern married her.

'Dag thee looks t'Kent,' was a Somerset phrase popular in the nineteenth century. Although it is insulting, it can hardly now refer to the ancient Kentish ruler, held responsible for letting in the invaders. Probably it just expressed regional exclusiveness, a minor but typical example of British insularity. Yet our studies of the folk song, the aspect of folk art which has most successfully transcended national frontiers, result from an event in Somerset, in summer 1903. It was in Hambridge, a few miles from Somerton, which echoes the county's original name, that Cecil Sharp heard the vicarage gardener singing 'The Seeds of Love'. The man's name was John English, which seemed well suited to the role that history gave him.

John Bull, another Somerset musician, achieved still greater fame, though his identification with the eighteenth-century caricature figure is mistaken. A tune of Bull's dating from the early seventeenth century, is the first real prototype of the national anthem, but, more pertinently, his distinguished career illustrates the triumph of personality over convention. Lacking a Latin education, generally a necessity for advancement in those days, he became an accepted member of contemporary intelligentsia, despite the additional disadvantage of west country origin. Scholastic circles then viewed regional speech with distaste, and Somerset dialect in particular retained many Middle English elements — some of them still persist. Alexander Gil, High Master of St Paul's School, observed (1621): 'Among all dialects, none is equal in vulgarity with those of the west; and especially if one hears the natives of the region of Somerset: for one may easily doubt whether they speak English or some foreign language.'

Today we know better. Kingsley Palmer worked for three years with the Institute of Dialect and Folklife Studies at Leeds University. He is a trained collector, and field work has formed the basis of much of his research into the folklore and oral traditions of the south-west. His involvement in adult education provided ideal opportunities for doing this and, since he himself was born and raised among the people of that area, he is excellently equipped for the task. Proof that this is so lies in the present book, a most useful addition to the series.

London University
November 1975   Venetia Newall

Introduction

FOLKLORE FROM the county of Somerset has formed material for literary works since at least the end of the seventeenth century, when Bovet talked of the fairies on the Blackdown Hills in his *Pandaemonium or the Devil's Cloyster.* Earlier writers such as Leland, Camden and Collinson were largely interested in history or natural geography and reference to the primitive beliefs of the country folk were cursory and not their main concern. It was not until the nineteenth century that writers began to consider folklore as substance for independent study, but there was still a tendency to include it, somewhat incidentally, with history and natural description. C. H. Poole made a useful contribution to the subject in 1877 with the publication of *The Customs, Superstitions and Legends of the County of Somerset.* Reprinted in 1970 the book provides valuable folklore material with some attempt at elementary classification. Other writers of the century were more copious in their matter, but included folk material as illustration or diversion from their main purpose which was the study of 'antiquities'. These included Boger in 1887 whose *Myths, Scenes and Worthies of the County of Somerset* includes numerous traditions collected from a variety of sources, and Walter's *Bygone Somerset* published in 1897.

The early years of this century gave us Hutton's *Highways and Byways in Somerset* (1912) which approaches to something near a travel book. The activities of the Somerset Folk Press must be seen as one of the important contributions to folklore collections in the county, with G. F. Munford's *Ghosts and Legends of South Somerset,* which, after Poole was one of the first books to be simply a collection of folklore material. The following year saw the publication of Mathews' *Tales of the Blackdown Borderland* containing a valuable collection of material from an area rich in lore, most of which would have died had it not been for the book.

There can be no doubt that the first serious work of folklore as we understand it today was Ruth Tongue's *Somerset Folklore* (1965)

14

edited by K. M. Briggs. The book utilized extensive folklore material collected by the author during her close association with the county. It was edited so that the material could be easily accessible, and, for the first time, every effort was made to ensure that sources and references were given — a departure that was long overdue in the history of recorded Somerset lore. Other books followed this lead. In 1973 J. Hurley published *Legends of Exmoor,* which included detailed material from the west of the county, and in the same year *Oral Folk-tales of Wessex* by the author of the present book included detailed material from areas in south Somerset. In 1974 R. W. Patten published *Exmoor Custom and Song,* which like Hurley's book included important data from parts of Somerset adjacent to the moor.

Of course there were other books and it is impossible to decide whether one was more valuable than another. All contributed in some way to the recorded lore taken from the county. What was primarily demanded was a thorough attempt to coordinate material collected so far, and with the inclusion of oral lore still there for the asking, to produce a book of Somerset folklore using exact standards and proper treatment of material that was both readable and a documentary record of what the folklore of Somerset was really about.

The information in this book comes from a variety of sources. The author undertook fieldwork in the south of the county, and much of what was collected in personal interview and discussion appears in the following pages. Informants were chosen for their knowledge and ability to contribute, and were given to understand that their names would not be used in publications. Thus notes for these sources appear as place names. Further details are available on request. The author came to live in the county in his early teens, and thus collected, sometimes unknowingly, material that has now been included in this book. Having been born in Bristol he also included material from the north of the county, remembered from that time. Bristol and the area of Somerset surrounding the city is not well represented in this book. Bristol would provide scope for a separate study, and there remains no doubt material in oral tradition in places like Cheddar, Blagdon, Mendip and Clevedon that is still uncollected.

Literary sources have been used where necessary, and in these cases reference is made to the fact in the notes. While the material in Miss Tongue's book has not been ignored, it is suggested that any student of Somerset folklore should also read her book, as this one is designed to continue the excellent work she began, and in no way supersedes it.

There were and still are a whole host of beliefs and half-beliefs that surround the activities of Somerset rural society. The first chapter is devoted to those that are 'popular', in that they occur consistently in traditions and involve frequently encountered situations or locations. Thus fairy lore is, or rather was, very much a part of popular lore, but this section of Somerset folklore extends to cover stories frequently told about buildings, stones and secret tunnels. The lore that deals with weddings and funerals is also dealt with in this chapter.

Many villages or churches have stories about their foundation and it appeared appropriate to set aside a chapter to consider this. Folk etymology, an interesting study itself, is also examined in the second chapter. 'The Daily Round' (Chapter three) continues the general lore surrounding society and settlement, and takes a look at those practices that in many cases are still observed. Naturally many of these customs are not limited to this county, a fact that applies to other material in this book. Lore was included if it was traditionally used or believed in the county, and folklore by definition is certainly not exclusive. However the Somerset housewife had to be as careful as any when spilling salt, or decorating her house. The chapter also looks at traditions concerning land tenure and candle auctions, as well as Friendly Societies that played an important role in the security of the rural community.

Witches were most certainly a more serious threat to the peace and tranquillity of the common man than they are today, when to call someone 'an old witch' is simply a term of disrespect. Chapter four and the two that follow it deal with the supernatural as it affected the lives of people. The ghost lore discussed in chapter six represents the largest and most popular body of tradition that survives in an ever continuing form to this day. It is interesting to note that while other beliefs tend to die — notably that in fairies — ghosts still haunt, and death threatens all. The fact that ghost lore, above all others, thrives and breeds in the dark lanes and derelict buildings is a serious comment on our progress.

Having dealt with the everyday and the supernatural it was appropriate to take a look at those seasonal customs, some of which are very much in vogue. Wassailing can still be found, as can the burning of the ashen faggot, though regrettably both customs are not as widespread as they once were. Clipping the Church appears to have survived up to the last war but is seen no longer, while May Day and the Minehead Hobby Horse still attract large crowds and the latter rivals Padstow as a folk attraction. Punkie Night is a tradition unique to Somerset, and has again received popular support and encouragement from local enthusiasts who certainly help to keep these customs alive.

Folk medicine is a mixture of magic, faith and popular science existing in its own right, and in some cases is still of importance. Chapters nine and ten deal mainly with historical matters, though the distinction is made between illegal activities, about which there is a considerable body of lore, and 'legend' or folk history. Interestingly enough much of the false information current amongst the folk, appears on further investigation to have been perpetrated by literary sources originating from those who should know better. A brief look at the humour of the county concludes the collection as a reminder that it was not all work and no play.

It will be observed that the notes for this book are set out at the end, and no numerical reference is made to them in the text. Every care has been taken to ensure that references can be easily located by the reader who requires them, and this departure is in no way designed to limit source reference or additional comment. The casual reader should find his task eased by not being obliged to devote his efforts to the pressing demands notes may make on his time.

No book is the work of the author alone. Thanks and sincere acknowledgement are due to many who have helped to make it possible. The informants, from whom this material was first collected, have really made this book, and I am grateful to them for their help and cooperation. The stories and myths told belong to the people from whom they came, and I trust that they will be satisfied with the way in which I have presented them with their own lore. Thanks are also due to my mother, Mrs Mary Palmer for all that she has collected on my behalf during the period of time I have been away from the county, and to Penny Taylor for her help and constant encouragement. Above all, I wish to thank R. W. Patten whose enthusiastic collection of material, and his generosity in making it available to me demonstrates his kindness and continual cooperation. I also wish to thank Venetia Newall for her many helpful suggestions, and to acknowledge her many alterations and emendations.

Finally I wish to apologise in advance to any who may feel that they have been overlooked or lack acknowledgement. It is difficult at times to ascribe an author to a particular tradition or belief. Suffice it to say that every attempt has been made to credit authorities and sources where possible and any omission on the author's part is regretted.

─○ 1 ○─

Popular
Beliefs

IN TRADITIONAL Somerset lore there were a number of beliefs that
did not in themselves form a part of everyday life. They were
beyond everyday experience, though they influenced and affected
behaviour and attitudes. In some cases the details of the belief or
half-belief became anecdotal; it was never long or sustained enough
however to become a part of the more substantial folk-tale except in
a few cases where it was worked into a narrative for entertainment
or instruction. Fairy lore interestingly demonstrates a body of lore
that is no longer a part of popular belief, but it has become
established as a part of the narrative tradition, and is now
maintained almost totally by literary sources. A few general
traditions persist in Somerset which could be called genuine popular
belief such as the fairy ring, where the fairies dance and where
mushrooms grow, and remnants of the 'pixy led' lore which used to
be considerable. Perhaps the sad state of fairy lore generally is
summed up by the following, collected from the Blackdowns in
1969.

19

> Fairies, now I 'eard something about 'em the other
> day, and you know, proper interesting it was too.
> Proper good story like they always is, always time
> for a good yarn like. Yes, twas on the wireless,
> you know, on that programme about the Archers and
> Ambridge, all about fairies. You should have
> listened to it, and then you'd have known all 'bout
> it and wouldn't 'ave 'ad to bother me.

Traditionally fairies are small supernatural folk, who generally do more harm than good, though their malevolence is usually confined to practical jokes. In a few cases they do cause actual injury. They are to be avoided rather than to be sought. The term fairy as opposed to pixy is a loose one. Traditions talk of the 'Fairy Fair', but of being 'pixy led'. Perhaps there is some inclination to think of fairies in a slightly more respectable light than pixies, though this notion is one that appears to have come from literature and not from popular tradition.

Perhaps the best known story of the fairies is that of the Fairy Fair. Its literary history dates back at least to 1684 when Bovet described one which took place on the Blackdown Hills at Blagdon. He calls the spirits 'Pixies': 'Their habits used to be of red, blue or green according to the old way of the Country Garb, with high-crown'd hats.' Numerous parallels can be found to Bovet's version, so that his makes an interesting narrative, and one can speculate as to how much it has affected oral tradition since that time. This is a paraphrase of his version:

About fifty years ago a person was riding over Blagdon hill, returning from Taunton to Combe St Nicholas. He saw before him what appeared to be a normal fair, and he took it to be Churchstanton fair that took place during that time of year. On remembering some story about fairies in that place he decided to ride nearer and take a closer look. However, though he could see well at a distance, at close quarters he could see nothing at all, only he was aware of a pushing crowd. He returned home, finding himself in pain. He became paralysed on one side, and remained so until his death many years later.

The tale is recorded by Poole, who contents himself with quoting Bovet. However by 1923 the story as collected by Mathews in *Tales of the Blackdown Borderland* has developed considerably. In this story the man is returning over the Blackdowns and sees the twinkling lights of a fair. Now, however, he was a man gifted with understanding of such events. He therefore went over to one of the many stalls, and asked to buy a pewter mug. He was not in the least perturbed to see that he was given several pebbles in his change. He went home, and found that the pewter mug turned into a puff ball, but the pebbles he had been given for change had turned into gold pieces. In such a story the pixies are in many ways less malevolent, and the tale contains the notion that if one treats the fairy folk with the correct reverence, all will be well in the end. Other stories have a less happy ending, though considering how the agent treats the fairies in the following account recorded by K. M. Briggs and R. L. Tongue in *Folktales of England*, it is perhaps surprising that he got off as lightly as he did. We are told how the man returning from market saw a pixy fair. He rode in and stole a gold mug which he carried away to his home. He put it for safe keeping in his bed, but next morning it turned into a toadstool. His horse was permanently lame. The story is also told by Ruth Tongue in her *Somerset Folklore*, along with another of a more careful farmer, who always left a plate of fresh water outside his house for the fairies, and a dish of scalded cream. However, one night he came across the Fairy Fair, and rode up to it, asking for a cider mug. This he bought, receiving leaves in his change. He politely went off saying nothing, and next morning the mug was solid silver and the leaves were lumps of gold. Such tales make a good introduction to the traditions of the fairies. The little people had to be treated with great respect.

There are a number of more general traditions concerning fairies. As their malevolent nature is well established it is not surprising that some concern the ways in which the pixy folk may be mollified. Thus it has been recorded from areas of Blackdowns that one should always leave some apples on the trees for them. This is known as a 'pixy word', or 'pixy hoard'. The pixies will then, in return, ensure a good crop for the following year. Such offerings have already been mentioned in the story of the good farmer and the Fairy Fair. However they are not limited to the Blackdown area. Mr J. Hurley tells us in *Legends of Exmoor* that it was the custom to leave a basin of bread and milk out as a reward for domestic chores that the pixies had done. They were also in some cases credited with finishing the threshing or cleaning up the home. Usually, however, they are responsible for practical jokes and social disruption. The offerings recorded here undoubtedly represent the remains of a much older belief in which the pixy was the representative of the Otherworld, and as a spirit had power over the lives of people. If directed to a good cause it could alleviate some of the natural capriciousness that was a part of the supernatural order of things.

A story that has been reported several times reflects the idea that the fairies were not always self-sufficient, and in fact sometimes sought the aid of human skills which they presumably lacked. The story of the fairy midwife illustrates this well. The fundamental outline of the story is as follows: 'A woman uses her skills to help the fairies. They grant her special privileges. She abuses these – loses them and perhaps suffers permanent damage.' As recorded by Briggs and Tongue, this tells how the woman rubbed her eyes with fairy ointment, bestowing the ability to see fairies at all times. As a result she was able to watch them stealing food at Taunton market, and scolded them. They turned on her 'like a cloud of angry wasps' and as a result she lost her eye sight. The story does not make it clear whether she lost her fairy eyesight, or whether she became blind altogether. Such permanent damage is not out of keeping with fairy traditions, but the story recorded by Mathews shows that the result was not always so disastrous. Mathews' version tells of a human nurse, who was approached by a pixy to help care for one of its kind who was sick. She received no payment, but was given pixy sight, and in addition prospered in all she did: her hens laid many eggs and her vegetables did well. However she too saw the pixies stealing from the butcher's stall down at Taunton market, and scolded them; whereupon she lost her pixy sight, but received no other damage, and continued to prosper. Hurley gives a version of the story without the nursing motif, and it demonstrates finally the dangers of crossing the fairy folk.

A woman at Minehead was said to have a male relative who had dealings with the pixies. One day she saw this relative in the market at Minehead, filching pieces of meat from the stalls. Going up to him, she said, 'Ah! I saw you.' 'Which eye did you see me with?' he asked. When the woman pointed to her right eye he blew upon it and she never saw from it again!

One of the most amusing groups of stories involves getting lost after dusk. Anyone who has walked on a really black night, with heavy cloud cover in woodland or along sunken lanes, will know that it can sometimes be very dark. Those who have tried to do this after a few pints of Somerset cider will appreciate that before the advent of the street lamp and the pocket torch it was not difficult to get lost, even in fairly well-known terrain. However the fellow who got lost was reluctant to admit to his incompetence. It was the fairies who were blamed for confusion and failure to find the way home. Being 'pixy led', as it was called, is a common tradition, and most small communities were able to provide their example of old so-and-so who got lost coming back late across the common. Needless to say, the strict tradition was altered when the power of the pixies came second to the mental disorders of the man lost. Most of the recorded stories are very similar, differing only in details of time and place. Suffice it to say that being pixy led had its remedy. If you turned your coat inside out, or even your pocket, it would break the spell. Presumably if you were unable to find the gate out of a field you might well be incapable of taking your coat off and turning it inside out. But, as Mathews reminds us: 'It takes a true native, they say, one of long descent in that region, or one of peculiar insight, such as some of these hill-folk are reputed to possess, to be favoured with a glimpse of these tiny sprites. . . .'

The traditions that deal with the moving of buildings from one site to another are sometimes connected with fairies. The supernatural agency involved may also be the devil or perhaps a named personage. Often changed site stories are told concerning places where the building (usually a church) is in fact a fair distance from the town. Alternatively the church may be now derelict, and the story explains why it is in such a state, blaming supernatural powers for its destruction. A few examples, collected from south Somerset will illustrate the point. The church at Broadway lies over a mile from the village. At a fairly simple level the story is given as: 'They tried to build the church up in the village but every night it was carried away – all built by day was carried away by night. That is why they built the church where they did.' Or: 'The church should be where the old Congregational chapel is now, but at night unknown people came along and removed the stones.' Other agencies mentioned by informants were the fairies, the druids and the pixies.

Similar stories are told about a church which stood nearby in the parish of Dowlish West at Moolham:

They built the church there, but the stones put up by day were taken down at night.

They used to say that what was built by day was knocked down at night, and had to be rebuilt. They used to say that it was the devil who had done this.

After the church was burnt down, what they rebuilt by day was carried back to Dowlish by night. The fairies must have carried it back.

The fullest and longest version of the tradition ran as follows:

They never built another church at Moolham. The story is that they tried to, but what they built by day was knocked over by night. They tried many times, but they gave up. The explanation was that the parish people of Dowlish did not want the church, because if there were two in the same parish, as there was before the fire, it meant paying more tithes. It was thus the people of Dowlish who went over to knock the church down.

The people, the old people, said that it was the fairies, or the pixies, and then people would say that it was haunted, and that you could never build there. All sorts of things are supposed to have been seen there. At certain times of the year, towards the end of summer, things are seen in the old churchyard. There is supposed to be a person in white who comes down through Kitchell's lane to the stream and disappears up the lane by the sheep wash.

The last account introduces much other material, but like so many traditions of this sort it emphasises the notion that the deed was done by fairies, ghosts or the like, that it was destroyed at night, and that there was a positive prohibition on rebuilding.

Allowenshay also had a church that is no longer visible, and understandably it produced similar traditions:

> There was a church just up the road ... but there are no relics of the place to be seen. It had been said that what was built by day was pulled down at night. It was not known who had done this, but it was probably the ghosts or something.

The tradition is not confined to south Somerset. Uphill church has a similar story associated with it, but the remover is unusual. The local school children have three balls on their school badges. These are the three bags of gold that St Nicholas tossed through the window to the poor people of the town. However he was less cooperative over the building of the parish church, which now stands at the top of the hill. Originally it was intended to be at the bottom. As building commenced, however, stones and timber were mysteriously transported at night up the hill, and while the workmen tried as hard as they could to assemble all necessary material in the right place, it was constantly removed to the very top. Eventually they realised that St Nicholas wanted his church built up there and that is what they did.

Secret passages or hidden tunnels are for some reason a widespread feature of popular belief. Most traditions are simple, with a statement about the existence of a tunnel. These would include the tunnel from Park Farm (Donyatt) to Ilminster, from Montecute House up to Ham Hill, from Gaulden Manor (Tolland) towards Wiveliscombe, and another towards the buildings of Grove Farm. The last example illustrates multiple tunnels, where the tradition exaggerates the number, and would have you believe that the place was honey-combed with them: 'There were tunnels from the church at Kingston to somewhere, but he and his friends did not know where. Certainly however one ran to Ilminster. There was a house in Kingston that had a tunnel to Dowlish Church.'

Sometimes a tunnel tradition carried with it a narrative which serves to emphasise the true nature of the statement:

> There were always supposed to be a great number of tunnels under the Court [Cricket Court, Ilminster] and they always said

that the previous owner, Sparrow, was able to get up onto Windwhistle to see the sun rise through one of these tunnels. There was also a tunnel from the Court to the Church. There is also a passage from the Rectory to the Church.

The story about this is that when the troops were billeted at the Court there was a parson called Oliver. The troops, Kent Yeomanry, were having a bit of a wild night, when the parson came right in between them, and they did not know where he came from. They supposed that he came in through the tunnel.

Hope of easy financial gain existed before the time of Football Pools and Premium Bonds. Folklore too contains the idea that money could be got without effort by more or less legitimate means. This often involved the fairies: Cadbury Castle is said to be full of gold which was put there when they fled from the country in ancient times. The church bells which they detest frightened them away. Such traditions usually add that the hill or mound in question is hollow, and there are details to prove it. Thus, in the case of Cadbury, the story is that there were once two wells, one on the hill's eastern face, and another on the western face. Its whole mass lay between the two wells. However, if you were to listen carefully by one wall, and get a friend to bang the lid of the other noisily, you would be able to hear him. Not only does the hill contain hollow chambers, but, as a result, the surface is subsiding. In the old days it was possible to see the top of the hill from the village – now you can see only the ramparts. Once a farmer planted a crop of barley up there but, when harvest time came, it had completely disappeared into hidden chambers.

There is a fairly well-known saying in Somerset:

> If Cadbury and Dolbury dolven were
> All England would plough a golden share
> [Or: All England would have a golden share].

However the treasure always remains unobtainable, often because of a taboo or rule that the treasure seekers do not observe.

Castle Neroche is a man-made mound, dating probably from mediaeval times. It was never, as far as we know, used for burials, nor did it contain anything of value. However, popular folklore has established around it a whole range of beliefs which particularly concern the earth work at its westernmost end. It is said to be hollow, and if you drop a coin down a rabbit hole you will hear it clink as it lands on the piles of wealth stored below. A ferret sent in after a rabbit will never be seen again, as it will get lost in the chambers beneath. Needless to say, there have been several attempts to find the treasure, all unsuccessful, and some fatal. The stories are still to be found in oral tradition.

They used to say that there was treasure in Castle Neroche mound. About forty or fifty years ago, six local people started to dig for treasure. They dug from the top, and the digging became very hard work. The diggers got annoyed and blasphemed. At once the hole closed in on top of them and half buried them.

There is a literary version of the tale, which probably developed from an actual incident which evidently appealed vividly to the folk imagination. In it the diggers were able to locate a metal box, but blasphemy caused it to sink from sight. After this, work became very difficult, and several bad accidents, thunder and lightning finally frightened them all away. They believed that the devil was up there and refused to go back.

The Quantock Hills also provide a similar tradition of buried riches. It is told of Broomfield, and states that beneath a certain spot there is a hoard of treasure, guarded by spirits, and protected by iron walls. The door to the fortress can only be located at full moon. Attempts to dig out the money have failed because of groans heard by the labourers, assumed to come from the spirits who guard the place. J. Hurley in *Legends of Exmoor* tells of a doctor who discovered the secret of the door through his skill and learning:

Late that night he returned with his servant and tools for digging, and eventually the spade struck on the iron door of the castle. At once horrid groans and cries were heard, and spirits began to emerge from the door. One caught the servant by the leg and would have carried him off, but the doctor put a Bible on the man's head and dragged him out and away with the other hand. The pit closed up, the door banged shut, and its position was changed so that it would never be found again.

Tumuli may also have similar traditions. These are more easily explicable since burial mounds did in fact sometimes contain treasure of one sort or another, and it is possible that the notion of hidden wealth stemmed at least in part from this knowledge. But the stories mentioned above, linking the treasure with the fairies, the traditional gatherers of gold, may also be relevant. Tumuli with treasure therefore illustrate one body of belief that, by extension, can include other mounds and lumps thought to be man-made.

Probably one of Somerset's best known barrows was Simons Burrow not far from Wellington, on the Blackdown Hills. It was said by Mathews to commemorate the stand made by Simon, Lord of Exmoor. He was killed and buried there. The earthworks remained until one James Bale, a road contractor, removed them in 1870. However there were originally two fields called Great Barrow Close and Little Barrow Close, and near to the road stood a great heap of stones supposed to be guarded by the devil. If any of the stones were removed he would bring it back. There was, so it was said, a crock of gold hidden beneath the barrow. While the devil and the fairies have not been doing their job very effectively, the tradition remains, particularly in literary sources.

Also on the Blackdowns are three tumuli known as Robin Hood's Butts. Collinson mentioned them, saying that they were traditionally the tombs of warriors who fell in battles between the Danes and the Saxons. The name is derived from the tradition that Robin Hood used them for target practice. There were originally five mounds, and the largest was sixty feet around. Naturally it was reputed to contain treasure and Bob Sims organized efforts to open it up. However the more they dug the less progress they seemed to make, and a stick driven into the ground to mark the day's progress would again be completely covered next morning. Finally the diggers became frightened and gave up. Today the mounds are very much reduced in size. Ruth Tongue has recorded a similar account, though the tribulations of the diggers were still greater. Finally the rich man who had financed the dig 'burst into tears, and no one has looked for the treasure since then'.

Standing Stones too have their stories of buried riches and man's frustrated attempts to dig them out. Near Castle Neroche is the small village of Staple Fitzpaine, where, until it was removed to make room for road improvements, there was a Devil's Stone or

Sarcen Stone. Apart from other traditions to be considered later, it was said to conceal a hoarde of treasure. This encouraged some locals to try and move it, but the stone was so heavy that one of them swore, which, as in the Broomfield story, put paid to the possibility. There were similar stones at Culm Davy and near Wellington. The first was supposed to have a huge crock of gold buried beneath it. An old man tried to excavate, but could not even reach the bottom of the stone. Someone else tried harnessing a team of horses to pull it up, but with no greater success, and the gold remained safe for ever. The Cock Crow Stone near Wellington turns every time the cock crows, and if you are lucky you can push it aside and extract the treasure. However, 'if it is not the right time or the right cock, you may push and heave for ever'. Another team of horses was tried on the Wimblestone in the Mendips but with the same disappointing result as at Culm Davy. The Caractacus Stone on Winsford Hill is another spot with similar traditions, but this appears to have been uprooted in 1936 and nothing of the sort was found.

Some stones simply move, without any associated treasure stories. When conditions are right they are credited with some such extraordinary mobility as the Ham Stone:

When Ham Stone hears the Norton Chimes at midnight clack
It rolls down the hill to drink at Jack o' Beards and back.

The Wimblestone at Shipham travels over the Mendips to the Westerstone at Wrington, and returns after quenching its thirst. Nor are such traditions confined to beliefs about stones. In the grounds of Hinton House there is a statue of Diana. It is told locally that, at the stroke of midnight, she descends from her pedestal to go for a drink of water.

Popular belief extends to buildings as well as to natural or semi-natural objects. At Langford church there is an unusual stone mark at the base of one of the capitals on the south arcade. It shows a needle, a foot long, and thread. Local tradition says that the church must have been built by a woman. The heads of the windows in the south aisle of Monksilver church show a hammer, nail, horseshoe and pincers. The story is that a blacksmith went to Bristol one day to buy a bag of iron. After obtaining what he wanted he returned home, but on opening the sack he discovered that by some mistake or good fortune he had been given a bag of gold. In gratitude he built the south aisle onto the church, and set his tool marks in the windows to show who had done it.

The tradition of Huish church tower has a less happy ending. The two towers of Huish and Kingsbury were built by an apprentice and his master builder respectively. When the master builder had finished he looked at Huish and saw at once that his own apprentice had made a better job than he had. In despair he threw himself off the Huish tower. Alternatively we are told that he threw down the apprentice — so the reader may choose which ending he prefers.

Some popular beliefs concern important stages of life, particularly the ones that are common to all men. Thus birth and death have a wealth of tradition associated with them, as do marriage and even divorce. In fact the last was not literally a part of tradition, but situations are embraced which would lead to what we know today as divorce. Birth was an important occasion, and what followed was necessary if the child was to have good luck through to adulthood. As will be mentioned again, a ginger-haired child was thought undesirable — though, short of dying the child's hair, there appear to be no remedies for this disadvantage. If the birth took place between midnight and cockcrow on a Friday the child would have special powers, enabling it to see spirits, to be beyond the power of witchcraft and to possess knowledge reserved only for these chosen few. A left-handed child will never do any good, so it must at once be taught to use the right hand.

Baptism is probably the most important single event following childbirth. It was believed that if a child died before this took place the spirit was destined to flutter for ever as a 'spunky' and would be seen as a 'Will o' the Wisp'. Alternatively they were said to be the moths that flutter at night about the lanterns. Christening was therefore something to be got out of the way as soon as possible, and, with an ailing child, this was often carried out prematurely. In south Somerset what happened on the way to the church was significant. The party proceeded with the baby, everybody dressed in their best. The leader of the procession carried some bread and cheese, and if they met any stranger on the way, he had to be offered some of this food. In return, he was obliged to give a penny and his acceptance meant good luck for the child. The coin was then preserved as a fortunate token. If the child screams at baptism, it is said that the devil has gone out of him; so, although babies are encouraged to be good in the church, folklore tells us that a yelling baby is desirable.

Even confirmation has developed its own lore. Poole tells us: 'Getting the left hand of the Bishop at confirmation is considered unlucky; and, when I was confirmed, I remember being warned by a servant to try and get the right hand. However I managed to get the left . . . much to her chagrin.'

Weddings were a great social event, and all the community was free to attend. Apart from earlier traditions associated with the event there is of course a continuing group of customs practised to this day. This is a traditional wedding song, which I heard as a child in north Somerset, though it was certainly not restricted to this location;

> Here comes the bride,
> Broad fat and wide,
> Into the carriage,
> And out of the other side.

Or:

> Here comes the bride,
> Broad fat and wide
> Six yards of muslin
> Wrapped round her hide.

The, 'something old, something new, something borrowed, something blue', and 'happy is the bride that the sun shines on' are both well known in Somerset, as is the custom of tying boots, tins and cans on the car that will drive the couple away.

However there are a number of customs that are of more specifically local origin. It has been recorded from both Huish and more generally from west Somerset that it was usual to place a rope of laurel flowers across the church path; the bridegroom has to pay before the rope is removed so that the couple may leave. At Hatch Beauchamp it is still the custom to tie the heavy oak church gates together, preventing the married pair from leaving until the bridegroom has struggled with the knots and got them open. One enterprising bridegroom-to-be went by night and removed the gates the evening before his wedding. They were well concealed, and he forgot about them when he left on his honeymoon. A few days later the vicar noticed that they were gone, and knowing that they were of considerable value told the police who agreed to investigate. They were replaced when the bridegroom returned, and heard about all the anxiety he had caused. In fact, undoing knots and getting married has some precedence in early belief, for it was the custom in some traditions for the bridegroom to undo all the knots in his bride's gown: otherwise she would not be able to conceive. Alternatively knots were known to prevent childbirth, and any knotted object was believed capable of causing the pregnant mother excessive pain until discovered and undone.

Divorce was out of the question in traditional folk life. Not only was it contrary to the law of the Church, it would have been financially crippling. Society also had its own custom for ensuring that a man and his wife were to some extent kept within the accepted framework. The guilty party was publicly ridiculed by a process known as Riding Skimmetty. In its milder form it exposed a man who was 'hen pecked'. The man was put on the same horse as his wife. He held a distaff, and his wife beat him with a ladle. There is a screen at one end of the Great Gallery at Montecute House depicting 'Riding Skimmetty'. However the crime was more usually adultery, and the accusation was made more realistic by the use of a puppet, which looked like the guilty party, and was known as a 'mommet'. It was paraded through the streets in a cart or on horseback, usually with the second wrongdoer similarly represented. The whole custom was accompanied by much noise from tins and trumpets. Hardy was familiar with the sanction and its abuse; he used it in *The Mayor of Casterbridge*. From Huish it is reported that a man whose wife had left him was ridiculed with a mommet made from a broom, which was placed on his chimney – it meant that he needed a new housekeeper, since the broom was the mark of her trade at hiring fairs. An informant from Muchelney remembered a woman being Skimmetty Ridden some eighty or ninety years ago for cuckolding her husband. A version of the same process has also been used within living memory to expose a bankrupt and a suspected homosexual. Skimmetty Riding demonstrated folk conservatism, narrowmindedness and the insensitivity of the group to the individual. It was used to maintain a rigid social order that had no room for the eccentric.

Death and funerals generate popular belief. In Chapter Three various portents of death are discussed, such as the howling dog and the cock crowing by night. A corpse was believed to be powerful. If you touched it or, better still, kissed its face you would not dream of the dead person. If somebody has difficulty in dying, the bed's stuffing must contain pigeon or partridge feathers. A murderer's remains are particularly effective in the prevention of certain illnesses, though any will cure swellings, lumps and T.B. The dead victim is also said to bleed when touched by its murderer. The story of Master Babb of Chard is fairly well documented. It tells how a criminal presented with this test, lost his nerve and fled. His guilt was thus revealed he was caught and finally hanged. The Somerset story of Jack White's Gibbet illustrates the same piece of folk belief, though on this occasion the corpse started to bleed when confronted by the murderer.

Burial was also most important. There were certain parts of the graveyard that were reserved for persons of ill repute, plague victims and the like. This was generally on the north side of the church, where the sun never shone, and therefore a cold place to lay a body. There is a tradition at Stogumber churchyard about a small triangular patch where there are no graves. Here it is said the victims of a plague were buried. There are also some remnants of the belief that each churchyard should have its guardian. This is a black dog, buried in the north side of the churchyard to keep the devil away. Ordinary interments should have the feet towards the east, ready for the Day of Judgement, but the vicar should face the opposite way, ready to address his congregation.

Malefactors were generally given no place in the churchyard, they were put at the crossroads with a stake through the heart to prevent them walking. Alternatively the Sexton might bury them in the churchyard, face down, to show which way they would go.

Black is the colour worn at funerals, though white was customary in the case of a child. A 'Cadbury Funeral' was one where the deceased was not likely to be much missed. Then the company would have 'dry eyes and wet throats'.

Popular traditions extend finally to areas of the unknown. To see into the future has always been one of man's great hopes, and it is not surprising that folklore provides numerous examples of people successfully foretelling certain events. In the following story, collected from Drayton in 1971, the prediction was made, and – despite efforts to avoid it – came true.

Brown's folly is a tower built on a hill on the Box (east) side of Bath. A local dignitary was told that his daughter would die on a certain day. So he built this tower with a room at the top, and had his daughter put in there. Food was sent up in a basket, and on the day that she was due to die, the basket came down untouched. Further investigation showed that she had died of snakebite.

A prediction made about Hinton House, Hinton St George is not quite so grim, but nevertheless contains the element of doom. It was said that:

> Hinton House is a dreary spot
> Hinton House will be forgot
> Here and there a shady tree
> And Hinton House will cease to be.

Recently the House has been sold. The park was divided and much ploughed up, and many of the trees had been cut down.

An often told story from Bath recounts how the Bishop, Oliver King, came to instigate the work on the west front of the Abbey. He dreamed that he saw the Holy Trinity with angels ascending and descending a ladder, and nearby an olive tree, on top of which was a crown. There was a voice that said 'Let an olive establish the crown, and let a king restore the church'. He therefore proceeded to execute his now famous design. The relative subtleties of the puns involved indicate that this is a piece of literary tradition which has since become a part of Somerset folklore.

2

Saints and Settlers

THERE ARE a number of folk traditions that deal specifically with early settlers or the origin of villages. They may tell how a place came to be where it was, and how it first obtained its name. Folk etymology is marked both by its imaginative qualities and by its basic inaccuracy. Many stories however are more ambitious, in that they tell in detail the events surrounding the lives of the first settlers. In almost all cases these were missionaries who introduced Christianity and so, according to present tradition, were the founders of the society to which the people owe allegiance. While folk etymology is very much a part of oral tradition, stories about saints and settlers are now almost entirely gleaned from literary sources. One suspects that the influence of the church through the ages has contributed to the miraculous side of the saints' lives, and the original volume of folk tradition is almost impossible to discover.

Folk interpretation of the origins of place names often rests on a pun derived from splitting the name into two or more syllables.

Thus from Dundry near Bristol comes this example recorded by Poole;

> Tradition asserts the name of this parish [Dundry] to have originated with the architect of the towers of Chew Magna, Chewton Mendip, and Dundry; on completion of the latter he is said to have exclaimed, 'Now I have *done dree*'.

Bleadon is supposed to have received its name from the time of the Danish raids that took place up and down the north Somerset coast. One one occasion, when the Danes landed, and set off to plunder and raid the land, an old woman cast their boats adrift on the fast receding spring-tide. Resistance was powerful and the invaders were driven back to the sea. Their craft were gone and they were slaughtered without mercy. The place was called Bleadon from that bloody day.

Sometimes a little learning is shown to be a dangerous thing, as with the supposed derivation of Norton Malreward. It is said that Sir John Hautville received the manor from William the Conqueror, but he considered it an inadequate recompense for his labours. He regarded it therefore as a 'Mal reward', a name that the place has had ever since that time.

South Somerset has its share of such place-name explanations. Whitelackington is reputed to have once possessed a white lake, and Seavington St Michael becomes the town (ton) twenty (vingt) miles from the sea (sea). In fact the name means the settlement at the locality of the 'Seven Wells'. Thus popular etymology was correct in its interpretation of a number, but it chose the wrong one.

The small village of Allowenshay obtained its name according to one informant in the following manner: 'The name came from the phrase, "Allowance of Hay". In the olden days, in the Monmouth wars that was the place where they rested, and the order was given that they should be given an allowance of hay.'

While the date of the wars varies from source to source the general explanation is the same. Others are perhaps even more far-fetched. Dowlish Wake is linked to Hereward the Wake, who, so the story continues, fled into the fen country and defied William the Conqueror. His descendants lived at Dowlish Wake. The derivation of the names is incorrect, so is the associated history.

Near Ilminster there is a place called Shave Lane. Its etymology offers perhaps the best insight into this level of erudition – inaccurate but compensated by its ability never to take anything too seriously: 'Shave Lane got its name because the monks had to shave before they went into the forest and up to the castle on the hills – which is of course Castle Neroche. They had to shave to make themselves presentable.'

Stories about saints are well documented and their place in present-day oral tradition stems largely from printed sources. Somerset has a good share and the better known must be included in any survey of the county's folklore.

St Carantoc is associated with Carhampton and his story describes how he had a remarkable altar that had been sent from heaven. Carantoc came to Somerset from Wales and the altar fell into the sea and was lost, so the saint went to Arthur and asked him if it had been washed ashore anywhere. It had in fact been found, but might not be reclaimed until the saint had performed a great deed – to capture the violent serpent that lived on Ker Moor. Carantoc, undaunted, placed his stole round the creature's neck and pacified it; then, ordering it to do no more harm, he let it go free. Afterwards he built a chapel for the altar which, so Leland tells us, was at Carhampton, though the church is not dedicated to him today.

Congresbury is said to have been founded by St Congar, or Cungar, who was the son of an Emperor or, according to Hutton, Prince of Byzantium. All versions record that he left there of necessity, some say because he wanted to avoid an arranged marriage, others because of a warning from an angel. He came to what is now Congresbury and established an oratory, so impressing King Ina with his great righteousness that he was granted land for his meditations. Tiring of the hermit's life he went on a pilgrimage to Jerusalem where he died, though his body was brought back to Congresbury and buried there. Bett tells us that when the saint arrived in Congresbury he planted his staff, which was made of yew, in the ground, and it took root and 'brought forth leaves', like the story of Joseph of Arimathea.

Watchet has a saint of some renown and he has given his name to the local parish church. St Decuman is said to have come over the sea from Wales on a hurdle, or on his cloak, accompanied by a cow that supplied him with milk. Despite these wonderful beginnings the career of St Decuman had its problems. He established a hermitage on landing, which so antagonised the local pagans that they decapitated him. But the saint's miraculous qualities were not confined to sailing. He simply picked up his head, replaced it on his shoulders and returned to Wales. Some say that where the head fell a spring appeared, now called St Decuman's well; according to other versions, it was already there when the saint washed his severed head in it. In either case the spring, still to be seen near the church, is credited with healing powers. The beheading motif and the associated spring is a relic of earlier belief and parallels exist in literature. However the story, as told in Somerset, appears to have been for the greater glory of the saint and his church. His festival is 27 August, and he is honoured, so they say, by a statue on the front of Wells Cathedral showing a man holding part of a skull in his hands.

Shapwick has its associations with Saint Indractus and his sister Drufa. The two were travelling to Glastonbury after a visit to Rome, their packs filled with millet and other goods for their journey, which would take them eventually to Ireland. They also carried brass-tipped staves. A party of servants belonging to King Ina saw the group, with bulging bags and what looked for all the world like gold-butted staves, and concluded that they were carrying bags of gold. They waited until both were lodged for the night at Shapwick, and then attacked, killing them and throwing their bodies into a pit. For three days after the murder a pillar of light shone over the place, so the corpses were discovered by the King, who ordered their removal to Glastonbury Abbey. Ruth Tongue adds an interesting piece of information: she says it is still believed that the light is sometimes seen over the place where the bodies were first hidden. This is a sign of approaching trouble.

St Dunstan is probably one of Somerset's best known saints. Historically we know little about him, except that he was Abbot of Glastonbury. According to Voragine's *Golden Legend* he took up office in AD 945. Most of the other details about the man really belong to folklore, though their existence owes more to literary sources than to oral tradition. E. Boger relates the saint's life in full, telling us that he was probably born in 915, of noble parents, near Glastonbury. As a boy he studied to excess and apparently made

himself ill. His first miracle was one of self-preservation: during an
illness he suddenly gained strength, went to the monastery church,
and up on the roof. He fell while walking along the beams, but
dropped unhurt into the aisle below. He was then sent to Court —
apparently to take his mind off his work. There he was soon
discredited by ill-wishers, and the King (Edmund, says Poole,
Athelstan, says Boger) dismissed him from Court. The resulting
story is well known. The King went out hunting, and in the chase
the stag leapt over a high cliff. Sometimes this is said to be Cheddar
Gorge. The King's horse was unmanageable, and the hounds too
excited. The whole pack careered over the cliff with the stag, and
the Royal horse was in imminent danger of doing the same. In the
nick of time however the King thought about Dunstan, and the evil
that had come to the man, and miraculously his mount stopped
short. Immediately on returning to court the King commanded that
Dunstan should be reinstated with honour and reverence.

A further miracle recorded by Poole is taken from Matthew of
Westminster. This time it involved Dunstan's mother, and
demonstrated what would be the future for her son. On the day of
the Purification Dunstan's parents were in the abbey. Suddenly all
the tapers that the people were holding went out, and everything
was dark, but the taper which Dunstan's mother was holding relit of
its own accord, and she was able to rekindle those of the others.

The association with the Virgin Mary and the regeneration of the
lights is a fairly obvious piece of ecclesiastical symbolism, doubtless
having its origin within the church. Perhaps this is also true of the
best known story about St Dunstan. His tempting has been seen as
an endeavour by the church to demonstrate how Dunstan dealt with
the corruption in monastic circles evidenced by history. Dunstan
appears to have spent some time working with metal, and one
evening, when he was busy in his workshop, the devil visited him in
the form of a beautiful woman. She said many flattering things to
him, and made provocative suggestions, but Dunstan realized who
she was, as he had seen a cloven hoof sticking out beneath her dress.
He happened to be holding a pair of red hot tongs and quickly
caught the devil by the nose. Despite his roars and cries Dunstan
would not let go. Finally the devil freed himself and dashed away,
complaining so loudly that all the town knew what had happened.
That Dunstan restored order and morality to the monastery is no

doubt commendable. However the legend omits to point out that the monks were as much — if not more — to blame than the women: the devil did not need to deny his sex to represent the truth correctly.

St Keyna was a virgin who lived in the fifth century and was responsible for the foundation of Keynsham. Before it was built there were numerous snakes, which Keyna miraculously turned into stone. The metamorphosed serpents can still be seen in the form of fossil ammonites. Collinson tells the story in more detail.

It has always been the popular opinion that Keynsham derived its name from one Keyna, a British Virgin who lived about the year of Christ 490, and according to Capgrave, a writer of the fourteenth century was daughter to Breganus, prince of that province in Wales which from him was afterwards called *Brecknockshire*. When the lady arrived at years of maturity she attracted many admirers, and many noble personages sought her in marriage; but she was deaf to all their overtures, having consecrated her virginity by a perpetual vow, for which cause she was denominated by the British, Keyna the Virgin. At length she determined to forsake her native country and seek some desert place where to indulge in private her religious contemplations.

Collinson goes on to describe how Keyna travelled beyond the Severn until she found somewhere suitable and asked the local Prince if she could settle. The prince was agreeable, but added that the place, 'so swarmed with serpents that neither man nor beast could live therein'. Keyna assured him that they would be no trouble, so her request was granted: '. . . by her prayers all the snakes and vipers were converted to stones. And to this day the stones in that country resemble the windings of the serpents . . . as if they had been so framed by the hand of the engraver.'

St Neot is another obscure saint, who nevertheless has a place in Somerset folk tradition. He was said to have been spiritual adviser to Alfred, though he is chiefly remembered for his miracle and his reputed piety. Like so many other saints, he apparently led a life of extreme deprivation and self-inflicted suffering, which was considered an important part of attaining holiness. The following miracle was recorded by William of Malmesbury some three hundred years after it took place. St Neot was at the time in a monastery, where he had the job of porter. At noon all the monks retired for meditation, and it was a rule that no talking or noise was allowed. Suddenly there was a loud and persistent knocking on the outer door, which was locked during their period of contemplation. St Neot had to open it, but found that he was too short to reach the lock and admit the person causing the disturbance. Apparently he did not have the stool on which he usually stood to perform such operations. Unperturbed, he offered up a prayer and the lock slid miraculously to a lower position where he could reach it. William of Malmesbury, who recorded the story, notes that he had actually seen the lock in this unusual position.

St Ulric led a rather uneventful life. His chief talent was prophesy and he was said to have been visited by both Henry I and Stephen; to the first he foretold death, to the second that he should gain the throne. It seems that he was originally something of a sportsman, enjoying hounds and hunting. But he abandoned these pleasures, and became very pious. He was born at Combe Martin, but spent all his life at Hazelbury Plucknett, near Crewkerne. It was there that he finally died and was buried, despite attempts by the monks at Montecute to have his relics removed to their own church. The traditions recorded about St Ulric are similar to those of St Wulfric, and it is probable that they represent the same person.

Perhaps the most bizarre of the Somerset saints, and in some ways the most traditional, is St Wigefort, known as Maid Uncumber. The little that is recorded about her does not suggest that she is peculiar to Somerset. However, the small church at Chew Stoke was originally known as St Wigefort's, although it is now dedicated to St Andrew. The saint, according to Bett, was the daughter of the heathen King of Portugal. She was converted to Christianity, but her father commanded that she should marry a heathen prince. Rather than compromise her religion by such an unholy union, Wigefort prayed that she should be delivered from her fate. She asked that her body should become disfigured in some way, so that the Prince would no longer wish to marry her. In due course she grew a beard, and presumably the Prince was dissuaded. Wigefort's angry father ordered that she should be crucified. Her reputation as a saint arose from these traditions, and she is portrayed as a bearded woman. But in popular belief she was revered by women anxious to get rid of their husbands, perhaps in righteous indignation, since the chief offering made to her was said to be wild oats. The name 'Maid Uncumber' thus explains itself. It is not easy to see how the 'uncumber' tradition developed from what was originally a virgin cult. St Wigefort fits into popular hagiography as the virgin who refuses every man for legitimate reasons and suffers as a result. Getting rid of an unwanted husband might have served as an important social safety valve in some instances, but it seems incredible that such obviously anti-doctrinal beliefs existed, and were permitted, with an actual altar in the church where wild oats were offered and husbands off-loaded. Unfortunately the exact details are not known. Perhaps the threat alone was sufficient. It is a part of traditional belief that once fulfilled an important role in the social structure. St Wigefort also had altars at St Paul's in London, and in St Mary le Port, Bristol.

St Wulfric has already been discussed as St Ulric, but many popular traditions are recorded under this first name. According to Poole St Wulfric was born at a place called Letona, about eight miles from Bristol. While in holy orders he kept up his hobby of hunting and seems to have been rather reckless. However, one day while out hunting he was asked to give alms to a beggar, and after that he devoted himself to a life of penance. He moved to Hazelbury Plucknett and there 'his fasts were continual, insomuch that he reduced his body to a skeleton, passing nights without sleep and even the little rest that he had was marred and rendered painful by leaning his head against the wall.' In the very cold weather we are told that he liked to throw himself into a bath of icy water, and stay there until he had recited the whole of the psalter. Wulfric could also cast out the devil's power, change water into wine, and is said to have fed forty persons from a small loaf of bread. Perhaps his best achievement was to reprimand a mouse that was gnawing at his cloak. The mouse ran to his feet and fell dead, – an object lesson to all its kind.

Not all early settlers were saints. Bath traditionally owes its origin to a pagan prince, Bladud who lived about 900 and was, according to Geoffrey of Monmouth, descended from Aeneas of Troy, and a great-grandson of Brutus. These comments underline the non-traditional nature of the story. Indeed the version telling how Bladud was a leper and discovered the hot healing waters as a

result has been variously told by several writers. His relationship
with Brutus is far-fetched, and he was also supposed to be
Hudibras' only son. Thus when it was discovered that the young
prince had leprosy, he was banished from the court. Prior to this his
mother had given him a ring, so that he would be recognizable to
her again – a traditional token found particularly in ballad literature.

Bladud went off to become a swineherd and led his pigs across
the Avon at Swainswick. Here he stayed for a while until his
attention was attracted by the condition of his herd, as the skins of
some of the pigs were becoming cracked and broken. All at once the
animals moved downhill to boggy marsh where there was a light
steam, and there they wallowed in what proved to be warm muddy
water. Miraculously, when they emerged, their skin diseases were
completely healed. Bladud followed their example, plunged into the
warm mud, and came out cured.

He returned to court, and made his presence known by dropping
his ring into a goblet. He was thus restored to his rightful place. The
rest of the story certainly does not belong to oral tradition, even if
the previous account ever did. Bladud travelled to Greece to study
literature and science, and appears to have become an erudite squire
– a foremost exponent of the sciences at that time. Indeed so eager
was he to encourage their progress that he one day demonstrated the
power of flight. Unlike Icarus he found that he had no power to fly
higher than his take-off point. Like Icarus he fell to his death, as
tradition has it, in his own courtyard. A lesser known story about
the prince is recorded by Warner in his *History of Bath,* claiming
that the local water there orginated from Bladuds' scientific
experiments. He buried in the earth two tuns containing burning
brass, and two of glass, containing seven types of salt, brimstone
and wild fire. These were placed over four springs, and by the
'fermentation of their contents' have caused, 'that great heat which
has continued for many ages, and should last for ever'.
Consequently, for a long time the waters were thought poisonous,
and not to be taken internally – a habit that did not form, according
to Warner, until the time of Charles II .

⟢3⟣

The Daily Round

THE PATTERN of rural life depends on a close relationship with the land, its flora and fauna, domesticated animals and cultivated ground. The house and hearth are centres for family activity, providing a sanctuary from the evils abroad after dark, and must therefore be made secure. Thus much general lore revolves round their protection from evil spirits. When erecting a house some care had to be exercised over the choice of building materials. An old lady from south Somerset told me once that she had as a child removed stones from an old church, long derelict. Her grandmother told her they were unlucky and must be taken back at once, or they would be 'fetched' by something less desirable, usually the fairies or even the devil. This belief did not prevent road builders from removing many of the stones from the Blackdowns above Wellington at Simons Burrow, – although ill luck is supposed to strike anyone who does this. Perhaps the old beliefs had more value than we realise. It has also been recorded that it was the custom to place a dead lizard beneath the foundations of a new field wall. On

Exmoor when a cottage was being demolished the bowls and stems of more than a dozen clay pipes were discovered. The informant inserted electric light bulbs, pieces of lead with his name and date scratched on and coppers into walls. He was not taught to do this, it just came naturally.

It is also very important to build the house in a suitable position. Some places are notoriously ill-omened, perhaps as the result of a murder, proximity to a gallows, or because the site has a long history of unhappy incidents, usually suicides. Such spots are avoided as house locations. Once the building has been completed several precautions are still necessary to ensure a trouble-free tenure. These traditions are fairly general and not confined to Somerset. It used to be the custom to place a bullock's heart, or even a piece of bacon, in the huge chimney. A pig's heart has also been noted; in one case over fifty were discovered in an old fireplace. To stick the heart with pins is an additional precaution, and, if the evil person is named while the pins are inserted, the magic will be the more powerful. This shows that it was often people or, more specifically, witches who were feared. I have been told that witchcraft was the problem, though a more general belief simply states that, 'bad luck' would result if a particular precaution was not taken. The chimney was an especially vulnerable part of the dwelling, as it could not be closed, like the door. The hearth also represented the centre of the home for it provided warmth, and originally light, cooked the food and kept things going maintaining the household. Hence it needed special safeguards.

The animals could be protected by hanging a stone with a natural hole on the cowshed wall. Such stones are regarded as supernatural. In north Somerset I was told that a seashell worn to the shape of a ring was prized above others.

According to Holinshed:

Some superstitious fools suppose that the cattle which die in the garget are ridden with the nightmare and therefore they hang up stones which naturally have holes in them, and must be looked for; as if such a stone were an apt cockshot for the devil to run through and solace himself withal, while the cattle go scot free and are not molested by him.

Probably the best-known household charm is the horseshoe, which must be placed the correct way up so that the goodness will not drain out. It is generally hung above doors. If one is found in a field, it should be picked up with the right hand and thrown over the left shoulder (north Somerset) thus averting bad luck and encouraging good fortune. It has also been recorded that the glass balls which fishermen used to keep their nets afloat were hung up outside a house to stave off misfortune. These were made at a glass factory at Nailsea.

Bad luck extends to a whole range of household occupations, and to the really superstitious there is almost nothing one can do without fear of some repercussion. A bird pecking at the window is a bad omen. You can expect a death if a picture falls down (sometimes also said of the bird at the window). A crowing hen is also unpopular; the farmer's wife should go out and cut off its head in order to avert disaster. A woman whistling is just as bad, thus we have:

> A whistling woman and a crowing hen
> Will fetch old Harry out of his den
> (Or: Are neither fit for God or men).

Hens roosting, during the day, are a warning of death. But if the cock crows at that time before the farmhouse door it means a visitor is coming. The cock crowing at night, on the other hand, is a death warning. A hen's nest should contain an odd number of eggs, otherwise she will not prosper.

A howling dog is a bad sign, and nails must never be cut on Friday, nor the clippings left lying about. Apart from being a tidy habit, this belief probably stems from the days when witches were a real force to be reckoned with, and it was a careless man who left nail parings for an ill-wisher to use against him in sympathetic magic.

It is said that if you accidentally smash one thing it will be followed by another breakage, though it is generally believed that one bad happening is followed by two more. Breaking a mirror is of course a well-known belief. So are spilling salt (throw a little over your left shoulder to frighten the devil away), thirteen at table and putting up an umbrella indoors. Tingling ears are a sign that you are being talked of: if the left ear, is affected it is a bad sign; but the right ear means something good has been said. The slander can be averted if the victim bites his little finger; then the ill-wisher will bite his tongue. Similarly an itching right eye is a good sign, the left is bad. If your nose itches you will be kissed, cursed, vexed, or shake hands with a fool. Perhaps the best in this series is an itching bottom, which, according to one source, predicts an increase in the price of butter. I have been told that salt on the front door-step will keep evil people away, and prevent them from calling.

Monday is the traditional wash day, but:

> Don't wash blankets in May,
> You'll wash a member of the family away.

You must not sing before breakfast, cross someone on the stairs, or put shoes on the table; no good will come of it. A hare crossing one's path is a bad omen, so is a black cat, – though a black cat can sometimes signify the opposite. It is unlucky to meet a funeral procession, but on seeing an ambulance or hearse, you must touch your collar until you notice a four-legged animal. Pouring tea from a pot that someone has already poured from means you will have a ginger baby; another version simply states that you will have a baby. Breaking mirrors, as we have seen, brings misfortune, but looking-glasses, presumably the smaller variety, are less disastrous. Instead of seven years bad luck, you lose a friend. Treading on a crack means your mother is screaming. But I remember, as a child, playing a game walking along the pavement in Bristol; if you stood on a crack, you had to say 'Bears'.

Removing a piece of loose cotton from someone's clothes signifies a letter, and pigs or rabbits should not be killed if there is an 'r' in the month, i.e. not before May or after August. Picking up a pin was also an opportunity not to be missed:

> See a pin and pick it up
> All the day will bring you luck
> See a pin and let it lie,
> You will want before you die.

Seeing the moon through glass, and more specifically the new moon, was thought bad, as is reversing any article of clothing after it has been put on inside out. To return to the house for something forgotten is best avoided, a belief that has also been recorded amongst miners in the north of England. Meeting a load of hay is good luck, but to look back at it is bad.

The list of popular traditions grows longer and longer. Somerset offers many simple sayings that are to be found elsewhere, and while modern education may eliminate some beliefs, modern communication certainly perpetuates others. These patterns represented an important part of the daily round, for they helped to order life's routine; it was by them that the day was judged, in part at least, a success or a failure.

Seasonal decorations are important, but no holly or mistletoe should be hung up before Christmas Eve, and everything must be removed before Twelfth Night. While hawthorn is taboo in the house may is allowed after 1 May. Some say ivy should not be brought indoors at any time.

The multitude of common beliefs are still important in the lives of some. Generally speaking there are more unlucky things you can do than preventative measures which can be taken against them. All forms of swearing were bad, and any work on Sunday could lead to the appearance of the devil. I was told about a woman who was working very hard, and she scrubbed the floor late into the night. It was Saturday, and midnight had passed before she realised. As she went to throw the bucket of water out of the door, she swore that the devil stood before her. He had come to get her for breaking the sabbath.

There was a tradition that the devil was unable to cross water, particularly if it was running, as this was thought to be specially holy. Further, water was believed to be clean and pure after it had flowed over five stones.

In times of inadequate ventilation, excess smoke was a problem. A small bundle of hay or small twigs, bound together and hung above the room, was supposed to purify the air by drawing the smoke into itself. It was explained to me that on opening the hay bundle after some time it was thick with yellow deposit and its efficacy thus proved. A 'No smoking' sign would probably be more effective.

There are a few general traditions of a more specialised nature concerning domestic activities. Bread-making took time and patience. It was said that you should never attempt it on a thundery day, or the dough would not rise. It was also thought that if it did not rise properly in the oven, the devil had passed over it. Cider was of course common in Somerset and the pleasure of drinking it, or rather what happens afterwards often figures in popular tales; but the actual process of preparation has produced surprisingly little lore. Nevertheless cider should not be made on 19 May, St Dunstan's Day. The saint is closely associated with Glastonbury, but his connection with cider is not obvious. Traditionally cider-making should start on All Saints Day, 1 November.

Other occupations generated their own beliefs. Thatching was one. Somerset has some fine examples of thatched cottages. The art, though no longer as important as it once was, continues in a small way despite rising costs. However a new thatch is expensive, good reed difficult to find, and it is only a large area that can support a single thatcher. The craft itself involves techniques that are beyond the scope of this book, but a small decoration is associated with the completion of a new thatch. Straw animals, pheasants, foxes, birds, or rabbits have long been regarded as suitable and are now sold for this purpose. A good traditional thatcher will often ask a house-owner if he may place a straw animal on the ridge of a thatch to complete his craftmanship. There have been various suggestions as to the meaning of this, and it is possible that in times past the decoration did have some spiritual significance. But if this was ever so, such a belief is now long dead. At any rate some thatchers do like to place these animals in a prominent position, even though they would say it was only a trade mark, or, 'It's nice to 'ave 'em up there'. The skill of making such objects is shared by the corn-dolly maker, though they are often one and the same person. But corn dollies will be discussed later.

Within the economic framework, tradition established ways by which land and titles are allocated. The daily activities were in some cases controlled by a structure imposed at regular and appointed times, which ensured the distribution of resources according to accepted custom. Somerset has a number of examples. Perhaps the most important business procedure on record is the letting or leasing of certain properties by means of the candle auction. This practice was not unique to Somerset, and an act passed in 1698 during the reign of William III permitted goods from the East Indies to be sold by candle. In Somerset candle auctions were known to take place at Tatworth, Chedzoy and Congresbury. The last one at Chedzoy was held in 1967, and the auction at Congresbury is long discontinued, so only the first is still observed annually. It takes place on the first Tuesday after the 6 April. The piece of land auctioned is known as Stowell Mead – a meadow and watercress bed. The ceremony takes place in the local inn. Only certain people have the right to attend the meeting. Usually it is those who own or rent property within the parish. The proceedings are timed by a length of tallow candle, about an inch long. It is hung above the table where it is invisible to the members, although they can see its reflection. The last to bid before the candle goes out gets the property for the year. Additional revenue is raised from fines for lateness, absence and other misdemeanours. Finally all monies are traditionally divided between the members, according to rights belonging to certain properties.

Records for the auction go back as far as 1832. It is said locally that previous records were burnt in civil disturbances. Thus the date and origin of the custom are unknown. In an article in the *Chard and Ilminster* newspaper (20 April 1972) R. W. Patten has pointed out that 6 April is Old Lady Day, a date clearly linked to land tenure. Lady Day (New Style) is 25 March and the twelve days between it and 6 April correspond to the period lost in 1752 when the Gregorian Calendar was substituted for the Julian Calendar. That being so, the auction would appear to be over two hundred years old – an implication that is not hard to accept.

At Chedzoy a piece of land known as 'Church Acre' is auctioned every twenty-one years. The candle auction dates back to about 1500, though there is some dispute as to the origin of the piece of land. Anyone may attend the auction, and the last, in 1967, was particularly well supported: the bidding went up to £204. The money goes to the building fund for the church.

A candle was not the only method of allocating land or rights. At Chard, on the last Thursday of October each year, the Chairman of the Highways, Tolls and Parking Committee auctions the privilege of collecting tolls from animals sold in the market, and from stalls and vendors working within the borough of Chard. The method of auction is a sandglass. When a bid is made the sandglass may be turned over on expiration three times; if no other bid is made, the offer is binding. The Borough holds a reserve price on the auction and if this is not reached the rights revert to the Council. Recently there appears to have been some trouble in finding any bidder to meet the reserve.

Congresbury also had its auction of land, though the custom has not been practised for many years. Ruth Tongue in *Somerset Folklore* states that the moors were enclosed in 1811, which probably ended the custom altogether. E. Boger also gives details of the auction which differ in some minor respects from Ruth Tongue. The land in question was known as East and West Dolemoors. Ruth Tongue locates it in 'the parishes of Congresbury, Wick St Lawrence and Puxton'; Boger in Congresbury and Paxton. A summary of Ruth Tongue's account is as follows:

On the Saturday after Midsummer Day those with rights to the moors go to Puxton Church to check the length of the special eighteen yard chain against an established distance within the church. Twenty-four apples were marked and an acre of land measured out by use of the chain. The moors were established in furlong units marked by posts. A boy kept the apples in a bag, and he walked round the moor drawing apples from his bag and marking on the turf the sign that it carried. Each tenant or owner knowing the marks and the furlongs belonging to his estate took what was due for the year.

Then all went to the Overseer's house for a candle auction of additional acres let to meet expenses. The auction was held in silence. Bidding was by picking up the last bidder's coin. This ceased when the candle went out. He whose shilling was by the candle had the land. This was followed by drinking.

E. Boger's account is briefer and clearer. I quote it verbatim;

On the Saturday before Old Midsummer Day, the several proprietors of contiguous estates, or their tenants, assembled at these commons, with a number of apples marked with similar figures, which were distributed by a boy to each of the commoners from a bag. At the close of the distribution, each person repaired to the allotment with the figure corresponding to the one upon his apple, and took possession of that piece of land the ensuing year. Four acres of land were reserved to pay the expenses of an entertainment at the house of the overseer of the Dolemoors, where the evening was spent in Festivity.

Neither version really explains how the land was divided, though it is probable that there were several areas of uniform size and the apple distribution meant that chance, or God, was the arbiter. It is of some interest that Boger gives the date as the Saturday before Old Midsummer Day. This auction therefore not only takes place in association with a Quarter Day, but a Quarter Day Old Style, thus supporting the view that these traditions pre-date the calendar change.

Farmers must have been those chiefly involved in such business transactions, and daily economic life in the rural community had its own traditions to be observed. A farmer in west Somerset was once noted counting his sheep. It had been a good lambing year, but as the sheep squeezed through a narrow gate to be counted, it was only the ewes not the lambs that were numbered. The farmer did not choose to explain his methods, but he was most unwilling to have his lambs counted, even though this would have provided useful information, as they were mostly to be sold later on.

'Stropping' or 'strapping' was a system whereby a farmer hired labour. According to this a set rate was paid to the worker per day, regardless of when he was hired. Thus a person who was hired early in the morning was paid the same as one hired just before lunch. This rather biblical system was apparently practised within living memory. Down at Taunton market 'luck money', as it was originally termed, was always paid to the agent, or to the person buying the stock. One pound above the agreed price was handed over, and received as a tip. The deal was not considered closed without it.

Traditions of economic structure included the prevention of serious loss by a system of social unions. The participants in these benefited mutually if prevented through sickness or other disability from supporting their families. The unions were known as Clubs, and are chiefly remembered for their annual rallies, known as 'Club Walks'. These were, as the phrase suggests, walks organized annually by the members, and usually included a church service in the morning, a lunch, preferably at an inn, and a parade through the neighbourhood, accompanied by a band and singing.

Most communities had a Club, and many are now no longer in existence. However, there survive observances of the annual Walk, marking the existence of an important part of social and economic daily life. The amount of money contributed varied from place to place. At Drayton and Muchelney the United Women's Friendly Society is still functioning and the fifty members or so now pay 10p (formerly 2s.) every three months. The money must be brought, as it is not collected, and if anyone is over three months in arrears she is fined 5p. When a member dies, her next of kin receive 5p per member as a legacy from the funds. The Club breaks every seven years and all the money in the fund, together with any interest, is divided amongst the members.

The Langport and Huish Club breaks every fifth year and the money is paid out. This Club holds its walk on the Saturday nearest the 29 May. The Drayton and Muchelney United Women's Friendly Society meets during the second week in June, and in 1973 Long Sutton Club was held on 16 June. The season for the Walk appears to be summer, though there is no consistency in the exact date.

Langport Club still holds its annual Walk, and while its other functions are now largely redundant, it remains as an example of what the annual Club Walk must have been like. Events started at about 8.30 a.m. with the members gathering and then moving off to the *Angel*. The Walk passed through the Council Estate, on to Court Field and then on to Huish Church for a service. Then they continued to the *Rose and Crown* for refreshments. Here a speech was made about the Club in the old days, and the band from Huish Episcopi played 'For He's a Jolly Good Fellow'. Finally the party returned to Langport and the *Dolphin* via the steep hill, visited the British Legion Club and ended at the *Black Swan* for a buffet dinner. Proceedings ended at about 4.00 p.m.

Important decorations for the Club Walk included the staves, which were carried by the officers. Unfortunately many of these have been lost, though local men who remember them say that they were about five feet long, with an ornamental head made from brass or some other metal. They were decorated with ribbon, which was often blue. Other Clubs were held at Curry Rivel, Barrington, Aller and Broadway within living memory.

Tradition and custom extended to man's relationship with the

animal world. Some were of a very practical nature, like 'bird
batting' to provision the larder. This involved catching small birds
in some numbers — essential in the case of sparrows, since a good
quantity were needed for an adequate meal. One informant
described the method as follows: 'You do get a gert net, zee, and
one of you 'old 'ee up bevore a bush, or on one zide of the ivy. Then
others, they do beat the bush on t'other side, and all the sparrows fly
into the net.' Another informant calls it 'bird baiting' and says it was
always done at night. Groups of four worked together, with a pole
and bell to startle the birds, a net to catch them, and a lantern to see
by. The dish which resulted took its place in the menu of Somerset
folk, and children would sing as the pie was put in the oven,

> The pie's in home!
> The birds begin to sing
> Isn't this a daddy-dish
> To set before a king?

At Huish it was customary to scatter a handful of grain at the barn
door to encourage birds, so that they could be netted. The nursery
rhyme acquires a new significance in this context;

> Sing a song of sixpence
> A pocket full of rye
> Four and twenty black birds
> baked in a pie.

The sixpence still needs to be explained. It is said that, when making
a rook pie, the birds' backbones had to be removed or the mixture
would not jelly properly; starlings were bitter, unless their necks
were broken.

Birds in general have produced a quantity of lore associated with
man's everyday encounters. Some of the traditions about the
farmyard cock have already been mentioned in another context.
Magpies feature in one of the best known sayings;

> One for sorrow
> Two for mirth,
> Three for a wedding,
> Four for a birth.

But it is unlucky to kill one. A single crow is also ill-omened and one perched in your path is a sign of bad things to come. An owl's screech is ominous too. The first cuckoo is an occasion for Somerset folk to turn the money in their pockets. Poole notes a song for the occasion;

Cuckoo, cuckoo, cherry tree
Catch a penny and give it me.

Robins are good birds, and it is very unlucky to kill one; the wren has the same reputation. There is a widely-known tradition, also found in Somerset, that the robin's breast was originally white. But it flew to Christ, bleeding on the cross, and since that time it has been red. Another version tells how the robin brought water in his beak to Christ during the Crucifixion and received his red breast from the Saviour's blood. The raven is badly thought of, though it is seldom seen in Somerset now. Birds with particular distinguishing marks were thought a good sign. One farmer mentioned a white rook and a white blackbird that he, 'liked to 'ave' on his farm. While it is true that black cocks were unpopular, I have not found this attitude much in evidence any more.

Animal lore is closely related to bird lore; once again some creatures bring good luck, some bad. Rabbits are regarded as a general pest, but the hare has greater importance. It is popularly associated with witches, and there is some evidence to support the view that it was worshipped in early times. Traditions from pre-Christian times may linger, though the association with witchcraft is more convincing in terms of oral continuity. The hare is generally regarded as lucky, though this may arise from the belief that the animal was in some way linked with witchcraft. Hence it was luckier to preserve one than to kill it. One farmer told me: 'Hares are nice things, I like to have one around the place.' A shrew mouse will die if it crosses a path but under no circumstances can an adder expire before sunset. Snakes have a poor reputation. It has been recorded from Huish that an adder and a viper are not the same: a viper has a 'v' on its head, an adder an 'a'. From the same source comes the idea that a fox cannot live twenty-four hours if he has lead in his flesh, and his teeth, being poisonous, infect any fowl he bites. So never eat a hen mauled by a fox. A vixen will not breed while her mother is still alive. A mole's behaviour provides information about the people in whose garden it is living. If it throws up numerous mole-hills, they owe money. Squealing pigs tell the same story – they have not been paid for.

Farmers do not like badgers, and tend to persecute them. The following story, given as it was collected, represents the animal in a more sympathetic light:

> There is a small country lane nearby [Staple Fitzpaine] called Badger Street. The old saying about how it got such a strange name was that all through the mating season of the badgers all the badgers from the Blackdowns used to come through Staple, and the ones from the Brendons used to come down the other way and they used to meet there and choose their wives. That is why it is called Badger Street. The ones from the Blackdowns were the males, and the ones from the other side, the Brendons were the females. Then at this place they would choose their wives for the season.

Horses are seldom mentioned in Somerset folklore. White ones are considered lucky in some places, though the good fortune is often dependent upon taking the correct course of action: 'See a white horse, cross your fingers and spit on them.'

Man's relationship with the environment has provided a rich flower lore. Beliefs relating more generally to natural objects sometimes suggest a residue from the distant past, granting them life, even a personality, of their own. Nowhere is this more clearly illustrated than with trees, whose characteristics and associations vary between the two extremes. The yew, traditionally the tree of death, is often found in churchyards. Collinson in 1791 explains that it was used in Somerset as part of the funeral ceremony. Branches were placed under the deceased, and, being evergreen, were, 'beautifully emblematical of the resurrection of the body'. This was most probably a christianisation of a pagan belief. Yew is popularly associated with the Druids, though, being poisonous, it has been said they were planted in the churchyard to prevent farmers from allowing their cattle to stray over the then unfenced cemetery. Oak and ash were generally regarded as benevolent trees, though even these could behave differently if badly treated. Ruth

Tongue tells a story about a wicked farmer and his eldest son who, because of their evil doings, angered an oak tree. The tree dropped one of its massive branches on the two of them and they were killed. Compare that story with the one about a man called Boilman, so re-named after being ordered to boil the quarters of one of his friends, who was found guilty by Judge Jeffreys during the Bloody Assize. Boilman was not beyond suspicion himself, and was given the task to establish his own good faith. Having escaped the Judge, he was saddled by his fellows with this new and objectionable surname. One day while out in the fields, he was caught by a great storm, took cover beneath a large oak tree, and was struck dead by lightning. The story does not make it clear whether the lightning struck Boilman, or the tree, but the implication is that the oak tree was more than partly responsible for dispensing justice.

Plants also have their own lore and associated beliefs. Parsley is regarded with some suspicion, and it is very unlucky to transplant it. The foxglove is the flower which foxes use as gloves. Wild orchids' leaves acquired their red spots when the blood of Christ dripped onto them as He hung on the cross. A good gardener will never let rhubarb go to seed, though I was not told what the result would be. The planting of seeds also has its lore: it should be done during a growing moon. In west Somerset 6 May is regarded as kidney-bean day, though the 1st, 5th and the 8th are also reported.

Any survey of daily life and its associated traditions would not be complete without an examination of weather beliefs. Many of these hold as good today as they ever did. Some deal with long-range predictions, such as the notion that if the churchyard is like a pasture at Christmas time, it will resemble a ploughed field come summer. The well-known rhyme about the ash and the oak is still told in Somerset;

> If the oak before the ash
> Then we'll only get a splash
> If the ash before the oak
> Then we're sure to get a soak.

It is also said that if there are plenty of good red berries on the holly at Christmas, the winter will be cold.

Often weather lore does not attempt such long-term

prognostications. The rhyme about red sky at night is too well
known to repeat, but there are a number of others. Traditionally in
south Somerset it is said: 'When the blackthorn comes out we do
never look for any nice warm weather.' When the skylark rises
straight the weather will be good, and when the sheep, stay down
on the grass till ten in the morning, it has the same significance. Rain
is a major concern of countrymen, and they say that it is on its way
when there is a small ring around the moon. If the new moon is on
its back, rain will come within twenty-four hours, but if it is upright,
the forecast is good. A mackerel sky is a well-known sign of bad
weather, though not for twelve hours after it has formed:

> Mackerel sky
> Twelve hours dry.

When sheep are noisy after a dry spell, the weather will soon break.
If you leave a rake lying downwards into the ground during the
hay-making season it will also cause rain, though if it is done by
mistake and you then curtsey to the sun, all will be well.

Perhaps the best weather prediction of them all is not confined to
Somerset but is certainly told there, often to unsuspecting
'foreigners': 'If you can zee the hills you knowz itz a goi' to rain. If
you cazun zee 'em you knowz it's raining already.

~~4~~

Witches and
Curses

THERE REMAINS one major difference between witchcraft and other areas of folk tradition. It is in the legislative control operated and persisting until comparatively recent times. Witchcraft was illegal like murder and other crimes which also have their own traditions and legends. Because of its real or supposed powers witchcraft had a very strong hold on the imagination of the people. Violent offences and any form of homicide were mostly unthinkable, but witchcraft was for many only too real. From the legend of the witch who was hanged locally, or the reputation of a woman who lived nearby, a self-perpetuating fear grew up. The church was also vehement in its condemnation of the black arts. Hence the occult has come to occupy a particular and important place in the body of folk belief.

As a result of the legal processes by which they were condemned there are any number of documented details about witches, how they acted and what finally happened to them. In so far as all witchcraft is a part of the study of folklore, these have their place in the present volume, and will be discussed below. The more traditional witch probably never reached such elevated heights, and existed locally within his or her own society, notable only in so far as they were held by the local residents in some sort of awe and respect. This leads to the inevitable question, 'What is a witch?' Within the sphere of Somerset folklore, it is a person who is reputed to have power over natural objects beyond that accepted as normal, and who can, at will, direct this power either for good or for evil.

From this it is clear that a witch can be either male or female, with either positive or negative influence, or even a mixture of both. While this is strictly true as far as definitions go, it is worth pointing out that most witches in both oral tradition and witch trials are female, and that the malevolent witch is far more frequently encountered than her opposite. Her benign counterpart usually has few tricks beyond curing warts and blessing cattle.

The witch assumed an important role in village society and usually operated freely, seldom interrupted by purges such as were experienced elsewhere. However the law was strong and a woman who overplayed her role could well find herself in a most uncomfortable position. The good, or 'white' witch acted simply as an advisor or doctor to the community. She was consulted on important decisions, cured illness, and countered evil from elsewhere. She was not feared, but was always treated with caution and respect. The self-appointed evil witch, or 'black' witch led a secluded and presumably rather miserable life, during which she more or less blackmailed the community. The contract was a simple one – hand out gifts to avoid being cursed. The fear that such a woman inspired throughout the village is an illustration of the importance of witchcraft in folk tradition. She was a parasitic element in the society, which very often fed and clothed her for no more than an assurance of safe conduct for them, their family and their cattle.

The importance of these activities in Somerset extended beyond the well-known witch. It was felt that the magic inherent in witchcraft would be directed to some extent by the layman. This invariably included evil procedures, where technique and standard practice were more important than belonging to any club. Thus sympathetic magic using a fetish, or even the more esoteric evil eye could be employed to a person's considerable and evil advantage. During times when superstition and the beliefs behind what is now euphemistically termed 'folklore' were real powers in orientating society, it was a serious accusation to blame a neighbour for illness or distress caused, as the Church would phrase it, 'by league with the devil' – in other words by witchcraft. In tradition we find therefore not only named witches, some of whom have been tried and executed, but local belief in old people who were thought to come within this category, charms to prevent their magic, and instances where the social situation has been upset by someone attributing blame for evil perpetrated in the name of witchcraft.

We will first examine witchcraft as a factor in local disputes. Several instances are recorded where a man has taken his neighbour to law over witchcraft accusations. Wyatt writing in about 1933 states that only three years previously a Huish farmer took another to Court over such an allegation. Unfortunately the result is not recorded. From Wadeford comes a story about the strife still sometimes noticeable between the village and Combe St Nicholas. The account concerned the informant's grandmother and grandfather. The grandmother had gone up to Combe St Nicholas and there met an acquaintance who was very agitated, claiming that the woman's husband had bewitched her, because on descending the stairs at midnight there had been a hook in the way. She was very frightened and upset.

Bewitching was always a part of everyday life, and the dishonest neighbour a potential caster of evil spells, so it is not surprising that Somerset folk had a wide collection of anecdotes and paraphernalia to counter such threats. General household charms have already been considered in Chapter 3, but there now follows a description of those relevant to the present context. The term for a puppet or small doll is a 'mommet' and it is used both as a fetish and as a counter charm. A small mommet placed near the door of a house would help to keep away witches, particularly if it was well treated and offered food and cider regularly. Such a mommet would probably have to be bought from a reputable white witch. If a pedlar had problems disposing of his wares, the threat of a curse would usually force a reluctant customer to do what was required. Someone who was clever could take evasive action by making a purchase with a silver coin, and smashing the object in front of the witch. This would destroy the curse. Of course it would have been cheaper to buy something for a farthing in the first place and so avoid the situation — but it was good to have the trick up your sleeve, just in case.

More mundane and respectable, is the belief recorded in south Somerset that a good Christian need not fear the effects of a curse, which is rendered harmless by the power of Christianity. Flowers also ward off evil. Garlic will prevent the evil eye. Mountain ash and bay are anathema to witches, so it is useful to have them growing near the house. Failing that, a bunch of rowan leaves tied to the head of the bed will keep away all evil. Juniper possesses similar powers.

Holy water is generally available and its use again illustrates the clash between the church and traditional witchcraft. Exorcism involving holy water can be used to counteract spells. Mercury or quicksilver was another liquid recorded as useful. A writer in 1922 noted an incident during his childhood, near Frome. A man came into a chemist shop and asked for quicksilver because he was bewitched. The chemist explained that it was very expensive, but on hearing the customer's problem agreed to sell him what he wanted. The trouble was that he could not sleep at night and was so frightened that he sweated and tossed about. He wanted to put the quicksilver in a small bodkin case, and tie it about his neck. The chemist also gave him some asafoetida to burn in his room, a substance that witches detest.

While there was certainly a hint of practical joking here, witches could be smoked out by using the correct ingredients. Hemlock, sloe rue and rosemary had to be dried and kept until May Day, and then burnt in the house by men who had been blessed by the vicar.

The decision as to who was or was not a witch appears to have rested more or less with the community, though animals are credited with powers of detection beyond our own, being quick to sense the supernatural. It was therefore possible for someone who was locally unpopular to be classed in this way, and even prosecuted as such mentally and physically, and there is no doubt that grave injustices were at times committed. However there were ways by which a true witch could be found out; the result no doubt of a feeling that justice was not to be done unless the crime was proven. The most popular method dates back to the middle of the seventeenth century when Matthew Hopkins was Witchfinder General. The belief was that if the suspected witch was cast into water her ability to float would be sufficient proof that she was a witch. This was because on making their contract with the devil they had renounced baptism, and it was therefore only logical that the water would renounce them. What happened if the woman sank is not recorded. Presumably if she was disliked enough it was merely concluded that she drowned as a good Christian after all. That such practices were employed in Somerset is witnessed by the following account quoted in *The Somerset Year Book* for 1922. The story concerns a village called Woodlands near Frome and took place in 1731.

... suspicion fell on a decrepit old woman living in the neighbourhood, and although the poor creature was suffering from ague, she was dragged out from her cottage, set astride a horse, and carried to a millpond about two miles away, where after stripping off her upper clothes, they tied her legs together, and putting a rope about her waist, threw her into the water, in the presence of two hundred spectators, who cheered and abetted the proceedings.

It was said that no amount of pushing would keep her under, but that 'she swam like a cork,' which, under the circ umstances was only natural, as both ends of the rope were held by some of her tormentors, and the slightest strain would cause her to rise to the surface.

When almost dead, they drew her to the bank, poured brandy down her throat, and put her in a stable, throwing some litter over her, where in an hour's time she died.

Although over 40 persons were concerned in this murder, the Coroner at the inquest could not discover the ring-leaders, as no-one could be persuaded to accuse his neighbour, so he was only able to charge three with manslaughter.

No doubt greater crimes have been committed elsewhere in the name of witch hunts and righteousness, but it sets the tone for so many of the stories about witches from Somerset. Underneath the folk beliefs and the fooling there is very often an old, lonely, mentally deranged woman, whose end could be nothing but isolation and misery.

The witch trial of the adult population spread down, to be copied by the children, who used it as a threat or a taunt to their peers. A child had to whirl a snail round at arm's length, to try and induce it to come out of its shell. The others meanwhile would chant;

> Snail, snail come out of your shell
> Or I'll kill your mother and father.

If the child was successful he was called a witch.

A witch was expected to make use of certain objects. Some of these, though popularly accepted, have no real basis in folk custom; the broomstick for example does not appear in oral tradition. Similarly the black cat is more often encountered in the children's story book than in anecdotes from the county. However, the belief that black cats are sometimes unlucky can probably be explained by its assumed association with witchcraft. Toads, on the other hand, are very much a part of sorcery, and are used by the witch in shape-changing, and spells. Ruth Tongue told me that as a child she went to visit an old lady who had dozens of toads. The little girl used to cuddle them in the middle of the road, regardless of the fact that their owner was a witch. Shape-shifting is an important characteristic of witchcraft, and it features prominently in many stories. But, as a rule, the witch chose a swifter-moving animal than a toad, since the transformation was usually to avoid the mob's anger. Thus the rabbit and hare were animals much associated with witchcraft, and white was a favourite colour. They therefore have magical associations.

No particular object appears to have been specifically used by Somerset witches in spells and curses. Drawing a circle was one technique. This encompassed the witch's power, and anyone entering it would fall under her evil influence. Similarly an imaginary line before the witch's house prevented animals from passing her door. The story as usually told ends with the witch not allowing a particular tradesman to go by until she has been given (or has stolen) some article she would otherwise have had to buy.

A witch's ladder was a powerful and useful device enabling her to enter any house or building. One was found in a house in North Street, Wellington, but the extent of their distribution is not known. Just how it worked is not described, though it consisted of a rope with a loop at one end. All through the rest of its length were feathers and thorns placed at irregular intervals.

Recorded witchcraft in folklore is divided between those instances where a witch is discussed generally, usually with an illustrative anecdote, and more specific traditions where the particular witch obtained sufficient notoriety to be remembered by name. General stories are by far the most common in Somerset and most elderly informants will tell you about old mother so and so who used to live up the lane, and everyone thought she was a witch. Other accounts are more detailed, and often include some material associated with witchcraft. Mathews records the following, which is unusual in that it tells of a male witch; 'There was an old man who kept many toads in his house. He could even turn into a toad if he wanted to do so. One day he was chased by a dog when he was a toad and caught by the leg. He limped for a long time afterwards.' From Bridgwater comes the story of a woman suspected of being a witch, and of changing her shape into a white rabbit. Someone in the district whose pig had been bewitched, went to the trouble of finding a remedy from a white witch. The suspect rabbit often ran down a certain lane, and the locals decided to get together and stop her activities once and for all. They laid in wait, and it was finally caught by the man whose pig had suffered. In his anger he kicked the creature, holding it by its ears as he returned to his companions in the hunt, but, before he rejoined them it escaped. However, the old woman was laid up in bed for three days after, unable to walk about.

A story with a similar motif is still told about the Black Smock Inn at Stathe. It was said that an old woman used to live in the house, who cast spells on the cattle and generally made a nuisance of herself. One day a group of local farmers decided that she had done enough and set out against her. She saw them coming, but was unable to make her getaway through the back door. Instead she went up the chimney, and ran off over the moors in the shape of a hare. However on escaping from the inn she burnt her smock, and the building has been named in memory ever since.

Somerset witches are numerous, but I will limit this account to those women, for all were female, who are better known, due to the volume of lore or documented evidence available. Mother Leakey was the subject of many accounts and even a Commission of Enquiry. She died in about 1634 but was soon credited with reappearing, and being something of a nuisance into the bargain.

Her son ran a shipping business in the Channel, and she was blamed for storms that finally broke him. She also strangled her grandson John in his cradle, but most famous of all was her encounter with the Minehead doctor, when walking in the fields. He treated her with some care, and even helped her over a stile. However, on approaching the next, she sat firmly on the top bar, and refused to let him through. He eventually managed to push past, but as he stepped down, the old woman kicked him on the bottom. This incident was the subject of a drawing by George Cruickshank (1792-1878) and Sir Walter Scott wrote notes about Mother Leakey in *Rokeby*, which shows the fame that the stories had achieved. The Commission of Enquiry set up to investigate the affair in 1637 was chaired by the Bishop of Bath and Wells. The Rector of Kingweston and Robert Phelipps of Montecute were his aides, but they appear to have found the evidence unconvincing, and the case was dismissed the same year on 4 February. However the tradition was not so easily got rid of and until quite recently Mother Leakey was blamed for bad weather in Minehead.

Mother Shipton was another well-known witch. She is associated in this area with Porlock and the Channel coastline. Her predictions chiefly consisted in forecasting tidal inundations, eventually of such scope that the spire of St Dubricius at Porlock would become a mooring post for ships. Further:

> Watchet and Doniford both shall drown
> and Williton become the seaport town.

According to Hurley, Mother Shipton was born in 1472 at Knaresborough, and married a Toby Shipton in about 1496. She lived until 1561 or thereabouts, and various places have laid claim to her grave. Her prophecies appear to have been popular, as they were sold in printed form, while she is remembered in local tradition by a few.

Joan Carne has a little more historical detail to support her existence. Besides, she has remained a well-known witch in oral tradition. The following story belongs very much to this, and was told to the author by Ruth Tongue:

An evil woman killed each of her three husbands. When she

herself died the local people were most pleased, and they put her in an iron coffin and buried her. However, when they returned home she was there frying bacon and eggs. They sent for the priest of Watchet, who was reckoned to be rather good; he'd finished off Master Lucket who had defied twelve priests. The priest exorcised her, and turned her first of all into a greyhound, and then sent her into the pool near Sandhill Manor. This is called the 'Witch's Pool' to this day. She cannot return except by one cock stride a year to Watchet church. She died something about 1606, and she should be back by now. Thus everyone is waiting for Sandhill Manor to burn.

In fact Joan Carne died in 1612 after burying three husbands – the last was Thomas Carne of Evenny, Glamorgan, the source of her name. There is no proof that she actually killed them, but traditionally she was credited with their murders, and so acquired the reputation of being a witch. One of the most popular and recurrent details of the story is that she was found at the Manor House cooking bacon and eggs. The exorcism took place during the last century according to one authority, though who the priest of Watchet was, and what had been his relationship with Master Lucket, I have been unable to discover.

Joan Carne was buried at Withycombe church, the building towards which, in most accounts, her gradual return is directed. The traditional measurement of a cock stride a year is shared with the Popham ghost. Sandhill Manor still exists as a farmhouse but the significance of the Witch's Pool has increased in the tale's telling.

There is a local tradition from Shepton Mallet concerning Nancy Camel. Nancy was reputed to be a witch, and was generally disliked. Her livelihood was knitting stockings, and evidently she earned the reputation of working excessively hard, even on Sundays, to make herself rich. She had made an agreement with the devil, though the details are not remembered or perhaps were never known. The day when the devil was to take her duly arrived, signalled by lightning and noise. All that was heard of Nancy was a shriek and a cry, and, when the inquisitive townfolk went to investigate next morning, her cave in the woods was deserted – doubtless to their delight. Clearly imprinted in the rock at its mouth were the marks of the devil's hoofs and the ruts of his cart as he carried her away to eternal torment.

Some witches have been buried at crossroads for obvious reasons. Near Ilminster is such a spot known as Mary Hunt's Grave, and it is sometimes said that she was a witch. Near Crewkerne there is another burial of this type reputedly that of a comparitively well-known witch. At a crossroads between there and Hinton St George lie the remains of Nan Bull, according to local tradition. She was generally thought to have been a witch, and one informant stated that she had been killed during a 'witch hunt'. Her full name was Mary Ann Bull, and she roamed west Somerset and Dorset in a little waggon pulled by a horse, trading in small merchandise. Though she was generally disliked and feared, it is difficult to say just how she came to be associated with the crossroads. She was well known over a wide area, and an informant of mine at Wool, Dorset remembered Nan Bull when he was a child. He added that she often used to camp in her waggon in a field near his home. O. Knot describes her as being rather too fond of drink, and cursing those she did not like. Spending one cold winter night as she was accustomed, under her cart, for she had no tent or other protection, the old woman finally died. An inquest was held at Wincanton, and that is presumably where she was buried.

Nan Bull is of interest because she represents typically the witch of popular tradition. Recent enough to be still a part of living memory, yet developed enough in lore to have a crossroads as her burial place, and in time no doubt, if conditions are conducive, elaborate traditions about her activities. Yet she was in her life time merely a social misfit, an eccentric, disliked and feared, mourned by no-one. Drink scarcely numbs a freezing wind on an icy night beneath a roadside cart; it is a lonely way to die.

Glanvil, a writer of the seventeenth century, tells us about Jane Brooks who was accused of bewitching Richard Jones in 1657. She gave the boy an apple for a piece of bread, and he soon afterwards became ill. Subsequently after eating the apple she had given him, which he had first roasted in the fire, he became worse. His father and others took action against Jane Brooks, said to have been an ugly hag. Incidents continued to occur, and the lad suffered acute pain. At one time he saw a vision of Jane Brooks, and a relative struck the wall at that point where it had appeared. Richard cried that he had cut Jane Brook's hand. Sure enough on visiting the witch they found that she had a similar injury, evidence which was conclusive enough for her to be hanged at Chard on 26 March 1658.

Glanvil also includes a confession by Elizabeth Style of Wincanton who was brought to trial with other members of a witch coven in 1664. Elizabeth Style had made a contract with the devil, who then appeared to her in the shape of a man, dog, cat or fly, and allowed her to harm anyone she chose, by making an image of the person in wax.

It is left to the tourist industry to promote a witch in contemporary tradition, as visitors to Wookey Hole will have discovered. There is a certain stone said to be the petrified remains of the famous witch of Wookey, who worked evil in the neighbourhood. She was turned to stone when a learned man sprinkled her with holy water. A visitor to the cave will also be shown various other petrified remains of her household apparatus. How old the legend is it is hard to say. William of Worcester writing in 1473 mentions 'the figure of a woman apparelled with a spinning distaff under her girdle', but does not say whether she was a witch. Bishop Percy in his *Reliques of Ancient English Poetry* (1765) may have been embellishing popular literature when he wrote of the witch of Wookey. He adds that the witch whose 'Haggard face was foull to see' left a curse on all the girls of the neighbourhood.

> That Wookey nymphs forsaken quite,
> Though sense and beauty both unite,
> Should find no leman kind.
> For lo! even as the field did say
> The sex have found it to this day,
> That men are wonderous scant.

The cure apparently lies in what follows:

> Come down from Oxenford, ye sparks,
> And, oh! revoke the spell . . .
> We only wait to find rich men
> As best deserves your choice.

It is hard to imagine anything further removed from witches and curses.

So that the balance between the sexes should be redressed, the final witch in this chapter is a man. Tradition might describe Sir Francis Drake as a 'wizard' but, despite his historical authenticity, his fame led many to think that his power was beyond that of an ordinary human being, and so he came to be regarded as a conjurer. Drake married the only surviving daughter of Sir George Sydenham, and it is this association with the Sydenhams and Combe Sydenham that links Drake so strongly with Somerset. The story tells us that after he became engaged he was forced to sail to the other side of the world, and so postpone his wedding. The family, growing impatient, agreed to the girl marrying another, and the arrangements were made. However Drake knew of the deceit, and fired a cannon ball half way round the globe which landed right in front of the bridal party. The incident was too much for the groom who fled, leaving Elizabeth Sydenham to Drake. The 'cannon' ball was for a long time in the house. G. F. Sydenham writing in 1928 says, 'In the house is still preserved the supposed cannon ball which according to legend Drake fired from the other side of the world.' More recently it was termed a meteorite, and was transferred to the Somerset Museum, though its true identity is, I think, still uncertain. It is said that the ball will roll in times of national crisis – perhaps by analogy with Drake's Drum; that it will always return to the house if taken away, a motif shared by stones of supernatural importance from ruins; and that it is tied to the leg of the kitchen table. The story is well known, and has been written about on numerous occasions. Sir Francis Drake remains firmly implanted in traditional folklore, supported on all sides by narrative accounts of his deeds as a witch, determined to have his own way.

⇒5⇐

Dragons Giants and Devils

DRAGONS, GIANTS and devils supplied solid material for folk tradition and it is in the anecdotal legend that we most frequently encounter them. In such tales there is therefore an element of entertainment, and while they are told ostensibly for enjoyment they mostly also have a more direct purpose. They explain the existence of some natural or unusual object by attributing its foundation to beings who were supernatural and possessed superhuman capabilities. They are also, with the exception of the occasional giant, about unpleasant events that were either feasible or had actually happened and are personalized only to the extent that a pseudo-human form is adopted. The atmosphere remains essentially supernatural, superpowerful and superbly malevolent.

Some of the lore concerning stones has already been considered in Chapter 1 but not all of them are associated with buried treasure. Standing Stones developed a sinister reputation, and there were all kinds of unpleasant experiences associated with them, the devil himself materialising, if time and conditions were right. There used

71

to be some stones along the roadside between Churchingford and Hemyock, and local tradition told of an old city called Cityford, destroyed in some war long ago. Some said that the stones were remnants of this. Whatever the reason, they had a bad reputation, and were considered 'troublesome'. One man claimed that he saw an animal like a calf emerge from behind and disappear into thin air.

The Standing Stone at Churchstanton was also thought to be uncanny. Late one night a group of girls had to pass it when returning from Baker's Farm. One of them thinking that the stories about the devil were mere ignorance, challenged him to appear as she went by. This he did, almost immediately, in the shape of a huge calf, which started to bellow. They all ran home as fast as they could and did not stop until safely indoors.

In both of these traditions the apparition has in effect been the devil, or an associated embodiment of evil. The lore dealing specifically with the devil and standing stones is considerable. However there is one story concerning an unusual stone on the Brendon Hills which omits Satan, but does include motifs encountered previously. The Naked Boy stands on the Brendon Hills where Old Cleve, Brompton Regis, Treborough and Withiel Florey parishes meet. It is said to be a metamorphosed drunkard, transformed into stone for his wickedness, who must go over the field every midnight as a penance to drink from a nearby spring. Metamorphosis is a fairly common result of evil ways or blasphemy, as is clearly illustrated in the traditions of Stanton Drew.

The following account comes from the *Western Flying Post* for 1 March 1813;

On the 20th ult. a poor woman in Milborne Port Workhouse, being charged with having a trivial article that was lost, wished God might strike her dumb, blind and deaf if she knew anything of it. About six in the evening of that day she ate her supper as well as usual, soon after which, awful to relate, her speech faltered, her eyes closed, and before seven she became a breathless corpse, without apparent cause.

An article in the *Taunton Courier* for 22 April 1857 tells of a foul-mouthed man who met his end in a shower of oaths. Entitled 'The Swearer's Prayer Suddenly Answered', it tells how two labourers at Glastonbury were unloading cinders near the railway station, and were swearing excessively. An embarrassed woman bystander asked the worst offender to moderate his language, but he simply swore that he would be cursed soon enough without his wishing it. At that moment the horse stepped up onto the railway line, and he attempted to turn it back.

A train, unperceived by him, instantly rushed up knocked him down, and the wheels running over him instantly killed him, launching him into the presence of his Maker ere his appalling oaths and curses had well expired upon his lips. And what is most affecting to relate, the aged man, his companion, stood over his mangled corpse as insensible and unmoved as a stone.

The theme of retribution is seen most clearly in these stories, although it does of course occur elsewhere. Standing Stones associated more specifically with the devil illustrate this point.

The stone at Culm Davey is known as the Devil's Stone, though it is more famous for its hidden gold. That at Staple Fitzpaine is referred to by the same name and local tradition associates it with evil. It was supposed to bleed if pricked, and to bear the imprint of the devil's fingers. A local story tells how the devil was sitting up on Castle Neroche, and saw the people of Staple Fitzpaine building a church. He was so cross that he threw the stone at the tower, trying to knock it down, but his aim was poor; it fell short, and has been there ever since. In another version he tried to roll it down hill to the church, but becoming tired, left it some distance from his goal. One informant claimed that there were in fact three stones:

They used to say that there were three stones called Devil's Three Jumps. The first of these was in Staple Fitzpaine itself. The second further up the hill, and the last towards the top of the hill. The devil had jumped from one stone to the next.

The stone at Staple Fitzpaine is now removed, and I understand it is the same that now stands in the grounds of Taunton Museum, safe from the road builders, and from oral tradition.

Broadway also has a legend about Standing Stones. The devil threw three stones at the local church, but missed, each stone falling

ITHACA COLLEGE LIBRARY

short of the mark. However, the people of Broadway moved the building further away, to where it now stands, just to be on the safe side.

Perhaps Somerset's most famous tradition of stones and devils comes from Stanton Drew. The megalithic monuments there are made up of three stone circles, a semi-circular arrangement of stones, and Hautville's Quoit. All these are situated in relationship to each other, and it is thought that they are contemporary. They probably belong to the Beaker period, that is between 2000 and 1600 BC. Naturally the existence of such a striking monument has stimulated legend. John Aubrey mentions it, acknowledging the tradition in 1664, and it has been retold many times since. The story in essence runs as follows:

A local couple got married on a Saturday, and held their wedding celebrations in the fields just outside Stanton Drew. As the dancing continued the bride became more and more enthusiastic about the entertainment. She was therefore most chagrined when, at midnight the fiddler who was providing the music, packed away his instrument and announced that, being now Sunday he would play no longer.

The bride was furious, but no amount of anger would persuade the musician to break the sabbath. As he went into the darkness, there appeared another musician, who said that he was willing to take over where the other had left off. He began by playing a somewhat slow tune, that did not please the bride. To please, he then played a faster tune, and all the company danced with energy and enthusiasm. In fact such was the speed of the tune, and such was the compulsion of the music, that none could resist it, and though they cried for mercy, could not stop their headlong flight. As the cock crew, the fiddler departed and as dawn broke the dancers no longer danced, but were turned into blocks of stone that remain there to this day.

The stones are known locally as 'The Fiddlers and the Maids', or 'The Wedding'. Details vary and one source adds that the wedding took place on Midsummer's eve, and that a cock crew, warning the dancers of the approaching doom at midnight. Another tells how it was a piper who provided the music on both occasions, and that the first and righteous musician stayed under the hedge, witnessing the whole affair. He was discovered half dead from fright next morning. All however agree that it was punishment for breaking the sabbath which caused the tragedy, that it was the bride who insisted on continuing beyond the midnight hour and that the devil himself led the dance in the form of a fiddler. The legend obviously has strong moralistic overtones, and the role of the bride suggests its masculine origin, though whether it reflects earlier beliefs is impossible to say. Whatever its basis, the story is very much part of the local folk tradition.

The lore associated with Stanton Drew is not limited to the well-known story discussed above. Hautville's Quoit has a legend of its own: the stones are locally supposed to defy counting. Wood of Bath wrote:

No one was ever able to reckon the number of these metamorphosed stones, or to take a draught of them, though several have attempted to do both, and proceeded until they were either struck dead upon the spot, or with such illness as soon carried them off.

A number of dialect poems, plays and songs have grown up from the legends; the most recent was published by *The English Folk Dance and Song Society* (Autumn 1971) and is sung by the Yetties on disc. One poem, composed in dialect in 1914 by R.R.C. Gregory has, Grinsell suggests, given rise to the belief current among school children that the wedding was between Kitty Stanton and Johnny Drew, though the E.F.D.S.S. version gives Sue and William. The tradition develops.

The devil was not always as active as at Stanton Drew, but his deeds are by no means limited to that district. Near Wellington it was believed that he visited the Wellington Monument every autumn after St Michael's day, the 29 September. After that date it is said that the blackberries are no good, 'vur the devil du spat on 'em ver spite'. The tradition about the devil walking over blackberries is widespread in the area, and it usually coincides with the first frost of the autumn which does indeed destroy the flavour of the fruit.

The devil is also said to be buried beneath Windwhistle. Here, so the story goes, he died of cold one winter, and now lies under the hill. His most famous contest however was on Exmoor at the spot today known as Tarr Steps. This is an ancient stone bridge over the River Barle, with slabs extending over 180 feet including the approaches. Tradition tells that it was built by the devil in a single night for his own use. On one occasion however a cat ventured across and was at once torn to pieces. The local priest decided to try the same, and as he did so, argued with Satan:

> *Devil*: You're a black crow.
> *Parson*: I'm no blacker than the devil.

The priest went over in safety, and after that the bridge could be used by everyone.

Giants were also given credit for the formation of natural features. One of the stories explaining the mounds known as Robin Hood's Butts, on the Blackdowns, tells how two giants used to throw mud at each other over a long distance. The Heaps were the result. At first they were rough and untidy, but after the giants' death they were smartened up. Where these giants were buried is not remembered, but a giant's grave near Bishop's Wood is still mentioned. In fact the site is the location of a now destroyed long barrow. The size of such mounds no doubt gave the impression that they contained a correspondingly large body.

We return to Stanton Drew for another giant. Maes Knoll, an earthwork a short distance to the north, was said to have been made by a giant's spade. However a local dignitary, Sir John Hautville, became incorporated into the legend. Hautville may have inherited an existing tradition, but was probably a big man himself; this, at least, is how he is recollected. He is said to have taken three men to the top of Norton church tower, one under each arm, and one in his teeth. The two in his armpits resisted and were squeezed to death. The other realised that it was better to keep quiet, and so survived, presumably to tell the tale. Clearly the giant was something of a local terror. He lived some time in the thirteenth century and is blamed for having thrown the Quoit from Maes Knoll. The stone has been much chipped away for road building.

Giant Gorm, the best known of his kind in north Somerset, was also responsible for forming the Avon Gorge. However he quarrelled with someone and was obliged to flee. He tripped and fell and his bones became Brean Down Flat Holm and Steep Holm in the Bristol Channel. Preserved in the rock at Blaize Castle are his footprints, which look quite realistic. Gorm's soap dish and his seat are perhaps less convincing. There have also been stories about giants from Dunster, the Quantocks and Exmoor. These are best read in K. M. Briggs and R. L. Tongue's book, *Folktales of England*.

Devils and giants made life dangerous in days gone by. In addition the folk had to contend with the occasional dragon; and Somerset has a number. On Stapley Farm, Churchstanton there is a field known locally as Wormstall. Here, long ago it was said that a dragon used to lurk, feeding on many of the inhabitants. Finally in time-honoured manner, a 'valiant knight' came to the rescue and slew it. The place where the monster died then became 'Wormstall' and the ground was furrowed by the lashing of its tail as it fought for its life. A hollow is still visible as a reminder of the incident.

The village of Norton Fitzwarren, not many miles from Taunton, has a well-established and particularly interesting tradition about a dragon, connected with the remains of an encampment dating from Iron Age, Roman and Saxon times. It is situated immediately behind the present town. The dragon is said to have emerged from the camp after a fierce battle. There were piles of dead bodies and, by a process not unlike spontaneous combustion they generated the dragon, which terrorised the neighbourhood, causing great damage and loss of life. It was again a local valiant, Fulk Fitzwarine, who came to the rescue, killing the monster and saving the people from further distress. It is possible that Norton Camp was attacked by the Danes in about AD 683, and the *Anglo-Saxon Chronicle* reads, 'Centwine drove the Brito-Welsh as far as the sea'. The argument from this follows that this means the country west of the Parrett along the coast to Quantoxhead. It is then suggested that, since the invaders supposedly used dragons as standards in battle, it was from this association of invasion, slaughter, defeat, and dragons that the legend arose. The brief and non-geographical entry in the *Anglo-Saxon Chronicle* is hardly grounds for assuming that Norton Camp was attacked by anyone at that date. Nor is there sufficient evidence that such invaders used a dragon as a standard. While neither is beyond the bounds of possibility we do have some reason to believe that dragons were used on standards in Wessex in 752. In the twelfth-century account of the battle of Burford by Henry of Huntingdon, Edethun preceded the West Saxons, 'regis insigne draconem scilicet aureum gerens'. Whatever the conclusion, Norton Fitzwarren has its dragon and it is commemorated on the very fine rood screen which survives in the parish church. The screen appears to have been the work, in part at least, of Ralph Harris, who died in 1509 and was buried at the west end of the building. He, or his helpers, decided to include the local tradition, so it was clearly well established in the fifteenth century. This much we do know. The relevant carving may be seen along the top of the main screen, and was originally brightly coloured. According to the church guide, these colours were partly eradicated in about 1825, when it was all covered with light oak paint. However, the colours do show through on close inspection with a strong light. A letter to *The Gentleman's Magazine* in 1829 describes the screen in its full glory:

The first dog is a greyhound, the other two are hounds, one yellow and the other black; next is a man in a yellow jerkin with red hose and cap, holding in his left hand a circular implement; he seems either on the point of falling a sacrifice to the monster which forms the next figure, or employed in attempting to entrap him. The animal is carved with great spirit, and is painted black with a golden stripe on his back.

A man is next represented with a bow in his hand and seems to be making his escape; he is dressed in red, with a yellow hat and shoes.

We have then three yoke of oxen dragging a plough, which is remarkable for the rudeness of its structure; the ploughman and driver are painted in a similar manner to the other human figures; next follows a seeds-man with his seeds-lip or box; the figure which is next is naked; and appears to be meant for a female; her hands are in the attitude of prayer, and she seems a resigned victim of the black monster which is in the act of devouring her.

It should be added that to the right of the dragon sequence there are three naked figures whose 'attitudes and employment', the writer to *Gentleman's Magazine* found, 'difficult to interpret'; but that was probably because he was a gentleman himself.

Not more than a few miles away, beneath the Quantock Hills lies the small village of Crowcombe, with a parish church containing some very fine bench end carvings. One, measuring about 10.5 in. by 1ft 11in. tall, shows two men destroying a double-headed dragon. It has small wings and a rather plump body, with a short, stumpy tail. The two heads are arranged one after the other, the neck continued out of the top of the first, up and forward, so balancing to some degree the symmetry of the design. The two men are indeterminately dressed. They look bored but businesslike as they assault the creature, which has a stick thrust in its lower mouth, and another in its belly, while the upper head and feet, oddly enough, seem to be taking very little notice. The whole effect is not without its appeal. No dragon story occurs locally to match the carving, though, as the bench ends are more or less contemporary with the screen at Norton Fitzwarren, it is not unlikely that the one influenced the other, or was even the work of the same artist. Ruth Tongue tells stories of dragons from Shervage Wood, which is not far from Crowcombe, and another, more monstrous at Kingston St Mary. This last was eventually killed by a brave man who rolled a great stone into his mouth which was open to roar, choking him.

Somerset's two remaining dragons belong to a rather different tradition for they both dwell in the marshes, and in shape and form were far more like serpents. In Chapter 2 we saw how St Carantoc caught and tamed the fierce serpent of Ker Moor, releasing it on condition that it did no one any more harm. Aller had a dragon that used to come out of the wild bogs of Sedgemoor. It devastated the neighbourhood, and for the local people life became intolerable, until a villager speared and killed it. The weapon was said to be at Low Ham chapel. Ruth Tongue adds that the beast came out of Athelney fens and the javelin, as she describes it, is nine feet long.

The Wild Hunt is sometimes mentioned in connection with fairies or the devil, but it should not be confused with either, or for that matter with ghostly riders. It consists of 'Yeth' Hounds and wild horsemen who gallop at a breakneck speed along given routes. To see or even hear them is particularly unlucky. Some say Triscombe Stone on the Quantocks should be avoided on certain dark nights when the Yeth Hounds are running. There is also supposed to be a wild pack near Watchet on Cleve Hill. Belief in the Yeth Hounds is well known in other areas both in Britain and

on the Continent. In Somerset it is often said to be the devil coming
to collect his own. When travelling at night it is advisable to ride a
horse with iron shoes, since they offer protection against evil spirits.
Failing that, if you run for your life and cross flowing water, you
will be safe.

The Yeth Hounds come from the Otherworld, and are
harbingers of death. Spirits and ghosts from the 'other side'
represent a vital tradition, and it is to the grave and its ghosts that
we must now turn.

⤜6⤛

Ghosts and the Grave

GHOST TRADITIONS represent a large and important part of folklore, and one that for the most part survives better than other folk beliefs. Most villages and larger towns have a hoard of these stories known to both old and young. Many concern important local buildings, manor houses and stately homes. To list all the available material from the whole county would be an immense task, so this chapter will discuss some of the better-known Somerset ghost stories, which represent a cross-section of the types most frequently encountered. Obviously, since ghosts are closely associated with death, burial, and the grave, these subjects often become a part of ghost lore.

While a house did not have to be of special local importance to possess a ghost, those that were of some standing in the community usually did. There was a house on the Taunton to Wellington road which attracted attention because it was isolated, the windows were boarded up, and it was generally in poor repair. It was said to be haunted by the ghost of a young woman who died of a broken heart after being jilted at the altar on her wedding day. Her wedding breakfast, so some said, was laid out untouched on the table, but it may be that this detail came from the obvious literary source. The building was pulled down during the Second World War.

Ilminster Girls' Grammar School was previously housed in the old buildings by the Minster. The famous old structure had its own story.

> One morning, early, before it was light I had to come to school, my father gave me a lift and he had to be in early. I went into school and made my way along a certain passage. At one end I caught a glimpse of something out of the corner of my eye. I turned round and saw at the end of the passageway, in outline in the bad light, the shape of a young girl. I was not frightened, but was surprised to see someone there at the time. Also, she had a long dress on, down to the floor – this was well before maxi dresses – her hair was all sort of spikey and not very nice. Later I mentioned this to a friend, thinking that it was very strange, and she said that she had seen something very similar, but had not liked to say anything for fear of sounding absurd. We mentioned it to one of our teachers, and she said that it was the ghost of a girl who died of diphtheria, who attended the school many years ago. Neither of us knew about the story before we saw the ghost. Apparently this girl caught the illness, and was in bed at the school. Her parents were sent for, but they were not kind to her, and were tardy in coming. When they did finally arrive, they were too late, and the girl had died. Her ghost still walks.

Large country houses are often haunted. Gaulden Manor, Tolland is no exception. The apparition of a small woman, appears on the front stairs – a grey lady who sits on the right of the fire-place, – and a ghostly coach can be heard outside the front door. Hinton House, Hinton St George has the spectre of a young woman whose lover was in poor circumstances. Her father, the Lord Paulett of the time, opposed the liaison, and the two eloped. It was not long before they were caught. Lord Paulett killed the young man, and his daughter died of a broken heart. She now appears, dressed in grey, on the grand staircase. The house has other haunted rooms, – one actually had to be closed as a result. Another, number 23, is known as the 'Ghost Room'.

The old vicarage at Cudworth is said to be haunted by the spectre of a man who was pushed down the stairs by his brother or father, and a figure in eighteenth-century clothing has been seen in the Grove at Stocklinch. Bardon House, in the parish of Old Cleve, has a number of ghosts, including a phantom coach, which is seen, not heard, and the image of a previous owner who walks the grounds of the house, his head under his arm. Inside harpsichord music has been heard at certain times.

The Garrick's Head Hotel, Bath, is reputedly haunted by the ghost of a man killed in a duel many years ago. Various landlords have experienced strange happenings, noises, objects being moved, and then reappearing elsewhere later. Tradition has it that the ghosts become more active when a new landlord takes over. The Theatre Royal, Bath has the phantom of a lady in grey, and other notable houses in the city with their ghosts are Citizens House, Combe Grove Hotel and dwellings in Grosvenor Place and Camden Crescent; the churchyard on London Road is frequented by a lovely lady who died in tragic circumstances. At Lansdown the cries and moans of soldiers killed in a battle during the Civil War may be heard on still nights.

Various Somerset notables are fresh in the memory of local inhabitants. King Arthur appears on Christmas Eve, riding along Hunting Causeway from Cadbury Castle to Glastonbury with his knights. Usually he is invisible except for the glint of his silver horse shoes, though the sounds have been heard by many. Sir George Sydenham's spirit is said to ride down Sydenham Combe, where the Sydenhams had long before made their home.

The most important Somerset ghost in this section is a contemporary of Sir George, Sir John Popham. According to tradition he was out hunting in a small combe about half-a-mile west of the Wellington Monument, known as Wilscombe Bottom. His horse stumbled and fell, and Popham was thrown into a pit and drowned. The pit was said to be bottomless. He was consigned to hell, where he would have stayed, had it not been for the good offices of his wife, who interceded with prayers. His ghost rose from the pit the following New Year's Eve at midnight, and advanced a cock stride a year towards the tomb of his spouse in Wellington Church. The process continued uninterrupted until 1859. A letter to the *Wellington Weekly News* on 23 June 1909

relates how fifty years earlier some men were cutting a tree in a
wood near the Monument. As they began to hew the trunk, it made
horrid noises, and pitiful cries. Such was its obvious distress that
they decided to postpone the felling for a couple of years. It was, so
they thought, the haven for Popham's ghost on his slow
cock-stride-a-year journey to Wellington Church.

Such an entertaining story needs further documentation. Popham
was an interesting character, and was not altogether well liked by
the local people. Born in 1531 at Huntworth near Bridgewater, he
was supposed to have been stolen as a child by gipsies. Whether that
detail is fact remains in doubt, though there is little uncertainty
about his early career in the study of law.

He was severall yeares addicted himselfe but little to the studie of
the lawes, but profligate company, and was wont to take a purse
with them. His wife considered her and his condition, and at last
prevailed with him to lead another life.

Aubrey, the author of these lines, is not alone in his condemnation of
Popham's early life. But it was his later success that was to damn
him as far as the folk were concerned. Apparently his wife finally
persuaded him to settle down, and his career after the 1570s was
entirely successful. He became a Speaker of the House of Commons,
and finally Chief Justice. His unpopularity with the people of the
county rested on the reputation earned after the trial of Raleigh,
Guy Fawkes and Garnet. Added to this, there was the unpleasant
affair of the Littlecote Estates. These passed to Popham soon after
the owner, Darrell, died. Darrell had previously been acquitted on a
murder charge brought before Popham, despite what was generally
regarded as damning evidence. Popham was depicted by Aubrey
and others as an unattractive man, 'huge as a barrel and grossly
ugly'. The combination of power, heavy judgements, doubtful
childhood and dubious youth, corruption and malice were too much
for folk tradition. His ghost was assigned to Wilscombe Bottom
and a bottomless pit, although in fact he died from a fatal disease on
1 June 1607 at the age of 72. He was buried in the Parish Church
of St John the Baptist, Wellington, and his elaborate tomb can be
seen in the south aisle.

Monmouth's misfortunes are remembered in the ghost of a man

seen at Catcott. In the churchyard there was an old building, in which it was said the Duke spent his last night before his defeat at Sedgemoor. A figure without a head walks at night in the area, though whether it is the spectre of Monmouth himself is not clear. Certainly local tradition has it that on certain nights the cries of the wounded may be heard on the battle field at Sedgemoor – a tradition similar to that already mentioned for Lansdown.

The majority of ghost stories concern local names and little-known places that have no place in history books or tourist guides. Quite small areas produce numerous ghost traditions, and dark lanes, deserted fields, old houses or desolate spots with a dubious past have their own wealth of such recollections. The variety of detail in each story adds to the complexity of the beliefs. At Duddlestone, near Corfe, there is a field where, on Christmas Eve at midnight, a headless man in a long cloak rides on a beautiful horse. Also at Corfe there is a story, still quite well known in the area, of a lady on a white mount who passes through a gate, crosses a field and disappears into the ground. On the Blackdowns there were once three brothers called Prowse. In turn they killed themselves, the first by cutting his throat, the second by hanging, the third by drowning. Now their house is haunted, and eventually the floor boards had to be taken up and replaced because of blood stains that could not be erased. A house at Henrietta Street, Bath, claims similar disfigurement, this time on the hearth, resulting from a wife's murder by her husband.

The landlord's eldest son at the Crown Inn, South Petherton is able to see the phantom of a woman burnt to death there during a fire at the turn of the century. This has been repeated during the tenure of the last three landlords. There is also the sound of a baby crying. A large, old house once stood at Horton Cross, on the A.303 a few miles out of Ilminster. It was burnt down and a new motel built in its place, so the resident ghost transferred to the new building. Whitcombe Terrace, Bath is haunted by an old woman, and there are the ghosts of little children dressed in white at White Hill, Huish Episcopi. In the Yeovil area there is a story about a phantom which helps itself to a pint of beer every night. In the old days, so they say, people who could not pay for their cider were locked up in the cellar of the pub. One night this happened to a man named Churchright, but there was a fire, and he burnt to death.

Since the pub was rebuilt, his ghost has made up for lost drinking time.

Another public house story tells of mysterious tapping at an inn on the Blackdowns. The ghost, known as 'Blue-burchies' from the blue breeches that he wore, was disposed of by two clergymen. They used bibles and candles to transform it into a horse. The animal plunged into a deep pool, and disappeared, but, as is common in these cases, it is said to be returning to the inn at the rate of a cock-stride-a-year. A local man told the following story of the Holman Clavel ghost:

Up at the Holman Clavel years ago, this place was sort of haunted, and this went on for years. It was nothing for them to hear the skittles in the alley, but when they went they would find nothing. At first the younger ones thought that it was someone playing about, but as it went on, and no one was seen, the older people said that it was 'Old Charlie' – perhaps an old man who had died, but who had stayed there. Further they would sometimes wash up the glasses at night, and leave them on the counter to dry over night to pack away next morning. Next morning they would find every cup put back in its place. The landlady began to find it all rather annoying, and could not stand it any longer. She thought that Charlie was turning up after wash day, as she had her clothes in from the line, and folded ready to iron. When she came in next morning everything was ironed and folded up for her. Though they tried to catch some one playing a trick they never did, and the old people used to say, 'It's old Charlie'.

When visiting the inn for a drink it is quite in order to ask how Old Charlie is doing.

Ghosts may assume a variety of forms, by no means limited to the human shape. Somerset folklore has examples of various animal ghosts and spirits, including the best known, Black Dogs. These are usually seen at night and haunt specific locations. To see them means bad luck, often death, for the viewer, or for a member of the family with whom the dog was associated. There are said to be Black Dogs at Westport, Dommett and Hinton St George. At Stapley a dog is reported with eyes as large as saucers. It is a sign of coming

bereavement to anyone who sees it. Another example is claimed for
Bishop's Lydeard. Snell, writing in 1903, gave details from
Thornton's *Reminiscences of an Old West Country Clergyman* of a
Black Dog seen by a traveller near Budleigh Hill. The local sexton,
on hearing this, explained that some time previously they had
brought a coffin that way, and the handle had worked loose. He
banged it in again with a stone, but presumably as a result a nail
pierced the skull inside. This allowed the spirit to escape, and the
Black Dog was the result. The corpse was being taken from Horner
Mill to Selworthy.

Phantom dogs were not always black. At Buckland St Mary, an
animal described as a cross between a donkey and a dog is
sometimes seen, and is usually white. Its appearance means that
some fatality will befall the owners of the Grange, Buckland St
Mary. Nor are animal spirits always dogs. Examples are a headless
horse at Foxenhole, between the hamlets of Marsh and
Bishopswood on the Blackdowns, and a ghostly sow and pigs
which materialise at midnight in Pay Knapp. A donkey has been
reported from near Cricket Malherbie and a spectral foal from
Curland.

There are a number of stories in Somerset folk tradition
describing someone's death as a result of folly and bad language.
Waterrow had a wicked squire who drank too much. He rode to
hounds frequently, swearing all the time, and boasted of his
contempt for the devil himself. One night he was returning from the
hunt when two stray hounds startled his mount. He swore and
galloped wildly across the common, but unluckily the horse fell,
breaking its own neck and that of its rider. Now the spectre of the
wild squire appears on New Year's Eve, going on horseback down
the road and over the common from Carriers Gate. The Hell
hounds chase from Young Oaks, where the steed was first
frightened, and accompany the ghostly pair until dawn.

In some cases the apparition is directly associated with a
phantom funeral procession. At Wood Court, near Ashill, six
phantom bearers carry a coffin up through Nunnery Lane to Ashill
Church. Similar apparitions are reported from Four Lanes,
Chilworthy and there is another on the road between Roadwater
and Golsoncott.

Much of the folklore connecting ghosts and graves develops from burial locations outside holy ground. Interment took place outside the churchyard for a number of reasons, the chief being suicide. Traditionally these unfortunates were refused burial in consecrated ground, and were denied Christian rites. Often they were put to rest at a crossroads, a stake through the heart. Both location and method aimed to ensure that the ghost did not 'walk'. How effective such procedures were may only be judged by the large body of ghost lore which has resulted from such burials. People who died without performance of the proper rites, who had been murdered, or who may have been outcasts in their own day, were also interred in unconsecrated ground. An Act passed during the reign of George IV laid down that the burial of suicides should be in a churchyard, or cemetery, and forbade the custom of the stake. As a result the north side of the churchyard was sometimes used. This area was thought unlucky and cold for the corpse. Traditionally it was reserved for the unbaptised. The lore surrounding crossroad burials survives, and those reputed to have a grave of some sort usually possess a ghost.

Between Wellington and Monument Hill there is a crossroads known as Webber's Grave. Webber was said to be a lawyer who robbed and cheated his clients. He finally killed himself because of his troubled conscience, and was buried at the crossroads nearest the deed. His ghost now haunts the spot. According to another version Webber was a sheep-stealer, but whether he died of a guilty conscience the informant did not know. The grave was apparently covered over when a new road was built. In the Ilminster area by far the most important crossroads burial with an associated ghost is that of Mary or Molly Hunt (see chapter 4, p. 68). Mary Hunt's grave is located where the road from Dowlish Ford to Cricket Malherbie crosses the road from West Dowlish to Knowle St Giles. Just who Mary Hunt was, or indeed if she ever existed, no one appears to know. Local information varies. Some say that she was a witch, others that she committed suicide because she was pregnant, while others claim that she was a prostitute. Whoever she was, she is said to have been buried by the crossroads, and some remember placing flowers on the grave in years gone by. Her ghost has been seen by local informants on a 'kind of trolley', on 'roller skates', 'riding a go-cart', 'doing her knitting'. A more traditional version went as follows:

At twelve o'clock at night you were supposed to see a ghost up there at Mary Hunt's grave. Mind you, I've never seen anything, and I've been up there at all times of night. I never saw one, or shaken hands with one. It was the ghost of Mary Hunt. She was supposed to have killed her husband out at Knowle. The villagers brought her up to the crossroads to bury her, and hanged her up as a sort of example to others. Then they were supposed to have buried her there as well, but I never dug for her. Between twelve o'clock and one o'clock Mary Hunt would rattle her chains — rattle her chains and turn in her grave. That's what they said, any rate.

Cannard's Grave is a much better known roadside burial place, though once again the history behind the tradition is confused. According to Poole he was a successful local landlord, but his avarice led him to commit a forgery. On being discovered he killed himself to avoid the consequences. He was buried in the usual manner at the crossroads nearest to the scene of his suicide, and since that time his ghost has walked in his old haunts.

The story of Jack White, and the gibbet that he now frequents, has already been mentioned. When he passed before the body of a murdered man, the corpse began to bleed. In folk tradition this meant that he was guilty of the crime, and led to his conviction. Hanged at the local crossroads, he was left there to rot, and his ghost now haunts the place, though it is not recorded what happened to his remains, when they were cut down. It is probable that he was buried by the crossroads. Ruth Tongue tells of a crossroads burial at Walford's Gibbet, on the Quantock Hills. Near Crewkerne there is an intersection known locally as Nan Bull's Grave. The circumstances of her death have already been described in Chapter 4 (p. 68), but local tradition knows better and consigns her to a crossroads which, she now haunts.

Various traditions exist concerning the burial of people within the churchyard precincts. At Stogumber churchyard there is a patch without any graves. This, according to local tradition, is where the victims of the plague were buried. Such an occurrence is not in fact beyond belief, and an additional piece of information from north Devon confirms the story. At Brayford there is also a part of the churchyard that is not used, and according to legend this again is the area used as a communal grave following an epidemic. In more general terms it is a Somerset tradition to bury unshriven persons on the northern side of the church, though the reason for this is not clear. It was, as already pointed out in considering suicides, 'cold' – that is, the sun obscured by the church building, actually shone on it a little, if at all. In a system of belief where the physical wellbeing of a spirit was of primary importance, it can easily be understood that this was an important point. It is also, according to local belief, the side on which a dog must be interred for protection against evil influences. Provided this has been done, burial on the site becomes acceptable.

The final aspect of ghosts and graves links the supernatural with the practical. Grave-robbing, like treasure seeking, has a very long history and dates from the period when corpses were buried with their wealth, which in some way they hoped to take with them. While potential grave-robbers realized the folly of such hopes, stories about their activities contain strong moral censure and sometimes consequent punishment.

Kentsford Manor, near Watchet is now a farmhouse. Previously a lady of the house, Florence Wyndham, fell ill, and was finally thought to be dead. She was buried in the vault of St Decuman's Church, Watchet, and left in peace. The sexton noticed that she had some fine rings on her hands, and was determined to get them. He went into the vault by night, and in attempting to remove them cut her fingers. To his consternation he noticed that blood was starting to ooze, and the corpse was moving. He ran out as quickly as he could. One version tells how he rushed in terror towards the sea, threw himself into the waves, and drowned. The woman got up out of the vault, and walked back home to join her husband. Of course she had never been dead. Poole indicates that the story may have had some foundation in fact. Presumably the robbery was added at a later date.

There are also tales of grave-plundering from Lambrook where an informant told of a similar case where a woman was dug up for her rings. However both this story and another from Seavington St Michael lack any details of retribution, though the second example does add that the lady woke, having been buried in a trance.

Unlike certain other aspects of folklore, ghost stories are very much alive and there is reason to believe that they will continue to develop in oral tradition. The grave still holds an important place in our thoughts and feelings; to most of us death is no less a mystery in the twentieth century than it was in the nineteenth.

—7—

But Once
a Year

THE PRECISE regularity of the recurring calendar provided a sense of security that has become as important as the seasons themselves. Indeed the two are frequently inseparable. It is small wonder that the change of 1752, with the omission of eleven days, caused considerable distress and, at least to some extent, was ignored in the celebration of tradition. Somerset is rich in calendar customs – and many of them are still observed – that are colourful, spectacular and usually much enjoyed by the participants. Others are less well known or are more or less forgotten. The dates are the skeleton of the folklore year; around them cling the meanings that make up the body of belief.

January

New Year's Day marks the beginning. The old year is left behind and it is a chance for a new start, a time to look forward. New Year resolutions are as popular in Somerset as elsewhere, and probably as ineffectual. They nevertheless are an indication of the desire to better the New Year and to ensure health and happiness in a fresh start. Traditionally, however, chance was thought more influential.

It was the man who first set foot inside the house on New Year's Day who shaped the pattern of life for the coming months. He should be dark, and carry a lump of coal. The custom was known as First Footing. Although the observance is generally practised in the northern counties, it is also a Somerset tradition and can still be found today. Needless to say, a dark man with a few small pieces of coal can visit his friends at this time of year and be rewarded for his efforts.

The uncertainty of the New Year is reflected in another custom which accepted the future as decided and merely attempted to determine its nature. This was divination by opening the Bible at random. It was usually performed at breakfast on New Year's Day, with all the family present. Each member would open the book and, without looking, place his finger on some part of the page. The verse selected in this way would then be read out and interpreted.

At Hambridge the first Sunday after Twelfth Night was and still is known as Plough Sunday. The plough is brought into the church and blessed, and this is looked upon as an important contribution to successful ploughing in preparation for spring sowing. There were also ploughing matches in various places, though the dates for these appear to have been variable. At Huish Episcopi the event caused quite a local stir:

> ... for a week beforehand harness was being cleaned, chains oiled and brass work polished (there were fifty brasses on the leading reins alone); and the chosen field on the morning of the match was a beautiful sight, with as many as fifty ploughs, each 'as long as a barn', drawn by a well groomed horse with bells and top-knots and beribboned tails, the brass amulets on the dark leather winking like jewels in the sun. The first prize was usually a gold watch; but the Jubilee match, which was won by a Wearne farmer, was open to all England, and the Queen gave a prize of money. Other usual prizes were a wheelbarrow for the best start, a whip for the best headland, a pair of sheets for the best bi-furrow; and when the same farmer's son, then a youth under twenty won his first match, again one open to all England, he took all four prizes at once – a Ploughing Match record.

January 6 was known as Old Christmas Day, and many people

declared that the calendar change had altered nothing. Old
Christmas Day was still widely regarded as holiday, and I have
been told not so many years ago that you would never expect to go
working on the farm on Old Christmas Day. It was a holiday and
made a natural end to the Christmas/New Year festivities. In this
case the original meaning of the date had been forgotten. Not so in
other traditions which stress that incidents imbued with mystical
significance still occur on that day, as if unable to adapt to a false
calendar imposed by mere human law. It was believed that the cattle
kneel down in their stalls on Christmas Eve. True traditionalists
state that this happens on 5 January. Similarly Christmas Day – 6
January by this reckoning – is the day when the white thorn at
Whitestaunton and West Buckland comes into flower. These holy
thorns were cuttings from the better known tree at Glastonbury.
The accounts usually involve failure of the thorn to bloom on
Christmas Day, as promised, but the disappointment is relieved
twelve days later on 6 January when the prediction is fulfilled. This
is supposed to illustrate the power of the supernatural and the
futility of trying to alter the calendar.

Twelfth Night is the final date for Christmas decorations to
remain. This appears to be modern folklore. Certainly in the north
of the county it was unlucky to leave decorations beyond that time.
In fact Twelfth Night was of some importance to the folk calendar,
and its significance long predates 1752, as we know from
Shakespeare's play.

The most important customs during the month of January are the
wassailing and ashen faggot rituals, which, although different
traditions, are often interrelated. Wassailing itself falls into two
parts; the wassailing of the apple tree, and the Visiting Wassail
when people are called upon and their health drunk. The dates of
the observance vary from place to place. Visiting Wassails are
sometimes associated with Christmas, though they usually take place
on Old Christmas Eve (5 January) or even Old Twelfth Night (17
January). For greater convenience it is often agreed to celebrate the
Festival at a weekend, so that the date becomes unimportant.
Perhaps this is because there is already considerable confusion over
the correct date, though the general time of year is established, and
is important.

The procedure for Visiting Wassails is straightforward. A group gets together on the evening of the appointed day, and visits various houses in the neighbourhood, where they are either sure of a welcome, or have made prior arrangements with the owner. The purpose is to propose the health of the householder, which is usually done by singing the wassailing song, and toasting the host immediately afterwards. Rewards are expected in the form of a tip, or liquid and other refreshment. Knocking at the door is not generally allowed, and the route is often arranged to include given houses and end up at the inn for the burning of the ashen faggot. This happened at Curry Rivel, where the two customs took place on the same evening. The Visiting Wassail is also observed at Drayton and Cecil Sharp collected one of many versions of the wassailing song from Langport. The words of the Visiting Wassail are of some interest. Local variations show the usual differences, and comparison with those Sharp collected generally indicate that the song has changed very little over the years. It is well known from primary school days and Christmas concerts.

> Wassail, oh wassail all over the town
> The cup it is white and the ale it is brown
> The cup it is made of the good old ashen tree
> And so is the beer of the best barley
>
> For its your wassail
> And it's our, our wassail
> And I'm jolly come to our jolly wassail.

The remaining verses often tell of a cow, or are more usually a direct justification for permission to enter the house and be rewarded.

The toast is traditional and simple, but needs to be heard in the thick rich Somerset accent to be fully appreciated.

> God bless Missus and Master and all the family.
> Wishing you a happy Christmas and a bright
>   and prosperous new Year.
> And many of them.

The Apple Tree Wassail also deals with the expectation of goodness for the coming year. It is still practised at places like

Carhampton and Walton, though there is evidence that it was more widespread until comparatively recently. Usually the oldest tree in the orchard is selected for treatment. The company gathers with the suitable paraphernalia and then makes its way to the orchard. Then a number of things happen. Shot guns are fired in the air, usually with some bravado, apparently to frighten the evil spirits. Toast is sometimes placed in the branches for the robins, and cider, sometimes hot and spiced, is poured round the roots. The tree is then 'wassailed', the company standing round singing the traditional song and invoking it to bear good apples during the coming season. A typical version would be as follows:

> Apple tree, apple tree we wassail thee,
> To bear and to bow,
> This year and another year,
> Hatsfuls, capsfuls and three corner sacksful
> And a little heap under the stairs.
> So holler boys, holler boys,
> Hip hip hooray.

Of the three customs the burning of the ashen faggot is the one that is still most widely observed. Again there is some variation in the date. At Buckland St Mary it was Christmas Eve, at Horton the turn of the year. In other places it was Old Christmas Eve, or Twelfth Night. The faggot was made of ash, and varied in size, though the more traditional versions appear to have been large, consisting of several dozen logs as thick as your arm. These were up to two metres in length. The faggot was bound together with bonds; these were of withy or hazel, though sometimes also of ash. The number of bonds varied; one, nine – three groups of three – and up to fifteen. Obviously the overall size was governed by the size of the fireplace, and traditionalists, limited by the scale of modern design, still burn a smaller faggot suitable for their reduced hearth. It is laid on the fire with due ceremony, and the company assembled at a private house or inn are treated to free refreshments. The festive atmosphere is encouraged by the drinking of a toast as each bond breaks in the fire. Consumption varies according to tradition; in some parts a pint of cider per bond is not considered excessive, so the whole evening is usually a great success.

February

Candlemas was an important date in the church calendar, for it is
the Feast of the Purification of the Virgin Mary. It falls on 2
February and is chiefly remembered in Somerset folklore for a
secular reason. Since the planting of certain crops was dependent on
the observance of traditional dates, church festivals were used as
reminders. Thus Somerset farmers advise planting peas or beans at
'Candlemas waddle'; that is, in the waning of the moon. We also
find;

> On Candlemas day if the thorn hangs a drop
> Then you're sure of a good pea crop.

February is likewise the month for Valentines. The 14th is still
observed and, now that we can buy mass-produced cards and
elaborate boxed hearts, the custom of sending your love a Valentine
is as popular as ever. The older customs have a certain finality about
them, since the Valentine that you saw first thing that morning was
the choice of your life. Perhaps we now have more opportunity to
experiment, though the Opies tell us that in Street speaking to a
person of the opposite sex before 12.00 noon was still regarded as
unlucky.

March

Lent probably affected the ordinary people as much as any church
observance. This was not only because of the inconvenient sanctions
it imposed, but because it prepared the way for a festival that had
both Christian and earlier significance. Nevertheless in traditional
Somerset terms it was the directives of the church that governed the
dates of the festivities, even if the actual customs themselves were
unorthodox. They began on Collop Monday, the day before Shrove
Tuesday, when it was customary to eat up all the meat in the house
– it was of course forbidden food in Lent. Shrove Tuesday was also
a day for overeating, though it is doubtful if all the pancakes made
the approaching period any easier to bear.

The simplest Shrove Tuesday custom involved eating pancakes in
private without any celebrations. But often the observances were a

good deal more complicated, and the customs that follow may have been observed in the whole or in part. 'Shrove' derives from the old English word *scrifan* which came to mean 'confess' – a very necessary process before Lent. Thus pancakes were the last treat before the coming austerity; the day had an almost holiday atmosphere. In northern counties it was a 'Mischief Day', though in Somerset it was usual to parade through the streets throwing broken pots and shards at doors and walls, to show, as one informant put it, that cooking was over until Lent was finished. This Lent Crocking – not to be confused with Lent Cocking, which will be discussed later – was frequently an opportunity for youths to pester the neighbourhood, making themselves a nuisance until the householder gave them a pancake to go away. The rhyme they chanted was:

> Tippety, tippety toe;
> Give me a pancake and then I'll go.

Clipping the Church often followed Pan Sharding, as Lent Crocking was also called. This was another preparation for Easter and Lent, the purpose being to drive out the devil. It involved a procession through the streets, when Lent Crocking might or might not take place. On arrival at the churchyard, the building was surrounded by the company who tried to encircle it completely, holding hands. If they succeeded the church had been 'Clipped'. Ruth Tongue informed me that Staplegrove Church was clipped up to the early 1960s, though the procession was orderly, and without the traditional dancing. In South Petherton, the people used to meet in the market place and parade through the streets to the churchyard where they blew trumpets. Hands were joined, and when the circle was complete, the trumpets were blown a second time. At Wellington the ceremony took place on Midsummer day, while in other places it occurred on Easter Monday. As with other customs already discussed, the actual date of observance of the custom varied considerably. Hutton gives one of the best accounts, from Langford Budville, where they have for centuries been endeavouring to frighten the devil away to the neighbouring village of Thorn St Margaret. The ceremony was performed on the Feast of St Peter and St Paul, 29 June. Hutton quotes from Professor Boyd Dawkins, and the description is worth including here:

Once every year the people met in the churchyard and formed a ring round the church. They advanced towards the church and on the side opposite the door the ring broke and the two leaders – something in the style of the dance, 'Sir Roger de Coverley' – went straight to the wall and were followed by the others. They then made their way back to the entrance to the churchyard and when they got there they gave three shouts.

Egg Shackling is comparatively simple, and is associated with Shrove Tuesday, though it was sometimes practised at Easter. It involved the shaking or 'shackling' of eggs in a sieve for a given period of time. Each had the owner's name inscribed upon it, and the winner was decided by the egg which survived the rough treatment intact. Alternatively they were rolled down a grassy slope to see which was toughest. The egg rolling took place at Triscombe and Stoke under Ham, where an earth work known as the Frying Pan was the scene of a stonemasons' picnic on Shrove Tuesday.

Lent Cocking is the most controversial of the Shrove-Tide customs. It seems possible that there has been some confusion between this event and Lent Crocking, though the origin of the former appears to be lost. In earlier times the holiday atmosphere was naturally conducive to cock fighting. Indeed there is good evidence to support this. Ruth Tongue told me that it was once the practice to shy at live cocks and when this was forbidden daffodils, which old people called Leny cocks, took their place. She also reports that a number of clay cock-shies were found in a Minehead house, which were used for Shrove Tuesday cock-shying. The subject could certainly be further investigated. There is also reference to the shying of a 'Jack a Lent', a small puppet, on Ash Wednesday, though the custom, as also some of the others, does not appear to have been peculiar to Somerset.

Ash Wednesday is the time when, dressed in sack cloth and covered with ashes, the faithful began their lenten penitence. However it is reported that in Somerset it was interpreted as *Hash* Wednesday, when Hash Meat was served up ceremonially and eaten. Ash Wednesday is also known as 'Cussing Day' since it was then that curses against impenitent sinners were read out in Church. The expected response was 'Amen', so people considered that this was tantamount to cursing your neighbour, hence 'Cussing Day'.

There is one further custom that frequently falls in March, and, rather like St Valentine's Day, it has retained its popularity in modern times. On Mothering Sunday it was traditional to take your mother a simnel cake, and the day is called alternatively, Simnel Sunday.

April

All Fools Day was and still is honoured in Somerset, the occasion to take advantage of other people's ignorance or stupidity for one's own amusement. The standard of jokes varied from simple fooling – 'Look, there's a spider right behind you' to more complex nonsense errands such as, 'Go down to the ironmonger's and ask for a pair of sky hooks'. Of course, fool's tasks are not restricted to 1 April. It was generally supposed that, unless completed by 12.00 noon, the joke was at the expense of the originator and 'April Fool' had to be shouted to seal its success. As a child in Bristol I remember jokes involving the telephone – you pretended to be someone else – and parents were persuaded to address envelopes to one's teacher, which were then sealed up with a piece of paper inside bearing the simple statement, 'April Fool'.

April 19 was generally honoured as Primrose Day, and it was customary to wear a primrose, or for children to gather them in bunches. Palm Sunday often falls about this time and it was then that some homage was due to the donkey, the beast that carried Christ to Jerusalem. April is chiefly the month of Easter, and while this is one of the most important and solemn festivals of the Christian calendar, the associated folklore is oddly ambiguous. Good Friday is a mixture of religious devotion and secular sport. Local children would go up to the hollow in the top of Brent Knoll that day, and have a picnic. Poole tells us that in some places on Easter Sunday it was the custom to climb the nearest high hill to see the sun rise, and that this ensured prosperity for the following year. Ruth Tongue confirms this custom from both Dunkery Beacon and Will's Neck. Easter eggs, like Valentine cards, have been exploited in the twentieth century, but they do reflect what was a traditional custom in Somerset, and elsewhere. Children decorated hens' eggs, and usually painted them with faces or other designs. It was also popular to boil them in water with various herbs, to impart a specific colour. Onion skin was perhaps the most usual; it turned the shell a rich yellow. Designs were sometimes painted on to this background.

May

May Day was always a great occasion with its holiday atmosphere, house decoration and, of course, the Maypole. It is not within the scope of this book to consider the original purpose of the Maypole, and much has already been written on the subject. In living memory it was always a harmless affair in Somerset, usually erected by primary-school teachers, and dancing performed by pretty children dressed in fresh, clean clothes. Many informants remember either taking part in these activities, or watching them on the village green. There is little doubt that they represent revivals of much older customs of a more adult nature, which Cromwell suppressed many years earlier. The 1 May also provided an opportunity for those with poor complexions, since May morning dew was particularly powerful and could even remove freckles. However it had to be applied before dawn, which required some effort.

The Minehead Hobby Horse occupies the first three days of the month and is a colourful and attractive spectacle. There are many views about the origin and age of the horse, but this discussion will deal with a description of what goes on now rather than what might have taken place in years gone by. The custom is not static, and variations in observances are common. There are sometimes as many as three horses, the Dunster Horse, The Sailor's Horse and the Town Horse. The models are similar. They are six to eight feet long and shaped like an inverted boat, with the wearer's masked head and part of his body protruding through the central section. The whole apparatus is supported by wooden formers, and is covered with cloth. The horse also has a long tail, an actual cow's tail, attached with a thick piece of rope. Gullivers, or rough attendants, accompanied the Town Horse, and the procession made its way through the streets accompanied by drums and accordions, shouting and singing; 'Soldier's Joy' was a popular tune. The Gullivers are allowed some licence, and were originally permitted to pass through houses along the route. It was considered bad luck to keep your door closed at this time. They teased bystanders, and encouraged them to give money, which was collected by the horse. A particulary mean person is 'booted' by the company, to the delight of all present. The horse's tail is quite dangerous; it is swung round with some force, and strikes any spectator who gets in the way. It is interesting that without exception all the informants who witnessed the more traditional hobby horse clearly remembered the stinging tail.

May Eve began the festivities with 'Show Night'. The procession visited the parks, and proceeded round the town where the main dancing took place. On this occasion and on most others it was the Sailor's Horse that was thought to be the original or 'parent' horse. At 6.00 a.m. on May Morning the horses go out to the crossroads at Whitecross. Naturally noise and uproar were very much a part of the Minehead Hobby Horse spectacle. Later it would appear, and make its way to Dunster, where it visited the Luttrells in the castle and was received with honour. On the second day Periton is visited, the following day Cher. The custom is flexible to the extent that the order of events varies from year to year, and from account to account − a factor that purists, who insist on the real tradition or nothing, might bear in mind.

The Minehead Horse is supposed to have driven off the Danes in the distant past − but then the Padstow Horse was supposed to have repelled the French. The similarity extends to the story of how the horses originated − Padstow claiming that Minehead stole it from Cornwall, and Minehead claiming that Padstow stole it from Somerset. It is interesting at this stage to mention nearby Combe Martin whose Hobby Horse did not survive as these others did, but was nonetheless important in its time. Somerset's surviving hobby horse is a relic of a custom once more widespread than it is now, and happily re-established for the present.

May 6 was known in the south of Somerset as Kidney Bean Day, and it was believed that, if you did not plant your beans then, they would not flourish. Later in the month, Oak Apple Day (29th) was known locally as Shik-Shak Day, when every one was obliged to wear an oak leaf. If you did not have one, you were known as a 'Jick Jack' and were punished accordingly. In parts of northern Somerset it appears to have been the traditional custom to substitute oak leaves for ash at midday, though more often than not the whole business terminated at noon. Other customs in the county include oak branch decorations and the slightly boisterous nature of a calendar holiday is often apparent.

June

Whitsuntide usually falls in June. Whit Sunday was an important festival, though the luxury of the Monday holiday was unknown in earlier times. On the Sunday it was customary for women to wear white ribbon in their shoes. Those who could not afford ribbon made do with white string or a white flower – a daisy would be an obvious choice.

June was also shearing time – hard, back-breaking work. Associated festivals are not very numerous, since sheep were never a dominant factor in Somerset's rural economy. However the successful completion of shearing marked an annual event. During the refreshments that followed this toast was offered;

> Here's health to the flock
> May God increase the stock
> Twenty where there's ten
> May we all come here
> Sheep shearing again.

A Christmas pudding was kept from December, specially for the occasion.

Midsummer's Eve was a favourite opportunity for divination, and for charming away evils. A holiday marked Midsummer's Day, and at Huish there were contests between opponents mounted on cider barrels and armed with staves. The first to draw blood was the victor and the festival was known as Stick Stack Day. Midsummer Day was also the occasion for clipping the church at Langford Budville.

July – August

These two months are a quiet period in the folk calendar. Naturally in good years the harvest might be finished by the end of August, and then the associated festivals would take place during that month. However it is more usually September before all is safely gathered in.

September

Special significance was paid to the last stook of corn brought in from the fields. At one level the occasion marked the successful termination of much labour, along with an end to the mental worry familiar to farmers, harvesting grain in an uncertain climate. As with some preceding customs it is all too easy to interpret them fancifully and give them an importance for which there is little firm justification. Certainly readers of Frazer find ample material for their conclusions. I have been told that the last stook was brought into the yard and placed on one side in a suitable place, where it remained until the following year, and it was then ploughed back into the soil for the next year's crop. The seed was mostly eaten by the birds in the intervening period. More generally the straw was used to make corn dollies – which, according to informed tradition, had to come from the last stook. Corn dollies really deserve a whole chapter of their own, though they are not peculiar to Somerset either in origin or occurrence. They represent a significant folklore survival, assisted by the folk craft of making the dolly – a much admired skill requiring patience and expertise. Contemporary designs range from the *cornucopia* to the cross, giving the interpreter a field day and the purist a headache as he endeavours to decide which were the 'traditional' forms – if ever such a thing existed. One informant told me that the dolly used to be kept in the church, until the following harvest was successfully completed.

But, more generally, local people stress the great rejoicing when the last load was brought into the barn. At Tatworth a lady remembered how the waggon was stopped half way through the gate of the barton and the men drank cider and blew on a horn. This is a typical recollection. So is the following description of the Harvest Supper – generally a Church event – which took place at East Brent.

The villagers process through the village to a large marquee, where a luncheon is held. At the end of the meal the local band plays in the puddings that the women bring in, and the men bring in a large loaf which six men carry, and a large cheese. The vicar cuts the cheese and the men scramble for the first piece that is cut.

The Harvest Festival church service is a traditional part of the Christian calendar, as is the Harvest Supper.

September 29 was a Quarter Day and was therefore a notable date. In Somerset it was the time to go out after crab apples, which were inscribed with the initials of prospective lovers and then stored in a dark place. They were inspected again on Old Michaelmas Day (11 October) and the initials easiest to read after that time were those of your true love. This custom seems to have been the prerogative of girls.

October

The two important festivals of this month are Hallowe'en, widely remembered throughout the county, and Punkie Night, an observance limited to a few places. It is still believed that witches are about at Hallowe'en and that it is a particularly dangerous time to embark on a journey. The festivities are generally confined to younger people, though Hallowe'en dances and parties are becoming increasingly popular with the adults. Younger people make lanterns from turnips or swedes. These are cut in half and hollowed out, leaving an outer case of about one quarter of an inch. The skin is then etched with a design representing a face, and a candle is placed in the lower half. The lantern is set up on a post or pillar, and used as a party decoration. It serves to keep away the evil things that are about on that night. The practice is fairly general throughout the county, though it has been particularly noted around Exmoor, south Somerset, – and the Brendon Hills, which are the site of another, rather macabre, custom. It is believed that on the night of Hallowe'en the images of all the persons who will die in the coming year pass through the churchyard. But, if the ghostly procession is disturbed, the watcher too could become a victim and be buried in the same churchyard within the next twelve months.

Punkie Night has certain parallels with the lanterns of Hallowe'en, but is credited with a different background. The custom has recently been observed at Hinton St George, mainly as a result of social organisation; it is also recorded at Lopen. The date varies. Generally it is the 28th or 29th of October, though recently, at Hinton St. George, the last Thursday in October has been selected. At Lopen the custom is more flexible, and is sometimes confused with the 5th of November, when the children beg for money for fireworks. The Punkie is a lantern similar to that made at Hallowe'en and already described. The main difference between the Punkie Night of Hinton and Lopen, and Hallowe'en as observed elsewhere, lies in the reason for the activities, rather than in the activities themselves. Both communities explain that the custom originated when the menfolk visited Chiselborough fair, which used to be held on 29 October, and having drunk too much cider were unable to find their way home. The women scooped out mangolds which were growing in the fields and, placing candles inside them, went out to guide their recalcitrant husbands home. The children now make them and traditionally proceed through the streets after dark, begging for money and chanting a version of a patter that generally goes:

> It's Punkie Night tonight
> It's Punkie Night tonight
> Give us a candle, give us a light
> It's Punkie Night tonight.

In another version Adam and Eve are mentioned and in a third a threat is made that if the candle and light are not given, then a 'fright' will be forthcoming.

Both villages claim that their custom was the first, and that the others stole it from them, an outlook we have encountered before. Hinton St George now makes it all quite an event, as these extracts from the *Chard and Ilminster News* illustrate:

Fifty children took part in the procession through the village, and the illuminated punkies were afterwards judged in the Victory Hall. . . . Thirteen children had been selling tickets to qualify for the honour of being Punkie King and Queen. . . . . HTV cameras filmed the Punkie procession and events in the hall including the crowning of the King and Queen.

The proceeds of the punkie celebrations amounted to well over £70 . . . the money will go towards providing a ceiling in the Sunday School in memory of a former caretaker.

So our untutored past adapts to our cultured present. The custom appears to be spreading. At Horton on 27 October 1972 there was a Punkie Night. It was organised by the village Sunday School and the children wore fancy dress and some of the punkies had beards and hair. After the judging, there was a parade through the village with music supplied by an old gramophone wheeled in a pram. In the same year there were similar evenings in Donyatt and Drayton. At Lopen, the event that year took place on 26 October and appears to have been organised by the children's mothers. There was no judging, but a spirited attempt to raise money produced 50p for each child taking part, and a variety of new designs on the lanterns including the simple engraved word, 'Chelsea'. The usual chant was sung and the penultimate line of one verse was, 'Ee-i-tiddlee-i', so I suspect the tune was 'The Farmer's in his den'. Apparently in the old days a mean householder was given a banger through his letter box – probably this would still be done, were it not for the mothers.

November

November 5 is a festival as popular as ever today but it is not restricted to Somerset, nor does the county offer any particular details lacking elsewhere. So it is enough to note the custom as an example of living folklore.

December

Christmas, the most important festival in December, makes a fitting conclusion to the folk year. Christmas Eve is a special time. It was believed that the cattle kneel down in their stalls as midnight approaches and it was customary to go to Church that night. The house was decorated with holly and ivy. Mistletoe over the door made it the place for a traditional kiss, a custom which happily survives, though the introduction of plastic reproductions in recent years can only be deplored. Christmas Day was, and still is, a time for eating and drinking, giving presents and relaxing. Entertainment from Mummers, once an important part of the occasion is something of the past. They performed a simple play, rehearsed for several weeks before, with a dance and an unsophisticated musical accompaniment. It is only the oldest informants who can remember these events, and it is a custom that has almost completely died out. Boxing Day was reserved for sports, particularly hunting. There was deer hunting on the Quantocks and Exmoor, with fox hunts or beagling elsewhere. For those who did not follow the hounds, Boxing Day was the time for rough shooting or trapping.

An Apple
a Day

'To eat an apple gwain to bed
'll make the doctors beg their bread.'

Wessex popular saying

FOLK MEDICINE reflects the ability of the rural community to deal with common ailments without recourse to doctors, and to survive without the scientific knowledge that was not then available. The validity of the following remedies is not really the question under discussion. For reasons, either scientific or psychological, certain remedies were adhered to long enough to become part of the county's folklore and this indicates their importance to the community from which they grew.

There are a number of general measures to be taken to avoid illness. An onion has long been considered a good cure. Halved and carried in your pocket, it will protect you from all ills, and hanging a bunch outside the door was supposed to keep away the plague. In

Tatworth there was a superstition that a small dose of Communion wine would protect the health of a sickening child but the custom was discontinued decades ago.

The most usual remedy for nettle stings was to rub the afflicted part with a dock leaf. This was highly effective when followed by the chant;

> Nettle out, dock in,
> Dock remove nettle sting.
> In dock, out nettle,
> Don't let the blood settle.

Asp and bee stings were rubbed with washing soda, a remedy that is, I suspect, a simplification of a pseudo-scientific home cure, originally recognising two types of sting, one acid, the other alkaline.

A common folk cure is for warts. These must be treated with respect since, if they are made to bleed, others will grow wherever the blood runs. The services of a recognised wart charmer are generally used to get rid of these growths. A charmer may have a particular system or he may, as a practitioner near Ilminster stated, simply 'think on't'. Results take time, and ring worm is said to be much easier. Some claim that a wart may be bought from another person, with a silver coin. In due course the buyer will see the wart begin to grow, as the vendor's diminishes. Alternatively, the purchaser discards the coin in a public place, and its finder rejoices in his good fortune without realizing that he has also acquired a wart to grow on him.

Rubbing with the inside of a broad bean pod, which must then be buried in the garden, is another wart cure; as the pod rots, so will the wart. Secrecy is often a necessary condition. From Drayton comes the belief that a wart painted with the milky sap of a garden weed will also disappear. In the Huish area the juice of crowsfoot is used, and a version of the broad bean pod cure substitutes an elder shoot, which must be applied to the growths. Notches are cut in the twig — as many as there are warts — and the process then parallels that with the pod. A similar and widely known cure uses meat in place of elder shoots. It should be beef and must be stolen. Corns, though they have inspired fewer remedies, are in some respects similar to warts. A pad of unwashed sheep's wool is one effective method. An ivy leaf bound in position will also cure them, and the same plant is used to benefit a cow off its food. A spray must be cut from among the top leaves, and the creature's appetite will soon return.

Boils were another nasty affliction which folklore could heal. The swelling had to be covered with a runner bean leaf, or treated with a poultice made from hot mashed turnips. Marshmallow leaves were also effective for this complaint. With a persistent sore, it was a good idea to apply the cream off the top of the milk while it was still warm, straight from the cow. Carbuncles are unlovelier than boils. A practical, if somewhat painful, remedy which also works with boils is based on contraction. Fill a bottle with hot water, and pour the water out. As soon as the last drop leaves the neck of the bottle place the rim firmly on the carbuncle. As the bottle cools it will contract, pulling the carbuncle out.

Styes are treated with a wedding or other ring, which must be gold; a remedy that is widely known and not confined to Britain. It should be used to stroke or even 'strike' the sore. Abscesses should be treated with a poultice made from groundsel, and chilblains must be rubbed with a tallow candle. Using only the most elementary resources, so many troublesome complaints may nonetheless be relieved if one only knows the secrets.

Accidents often result in bleeding, or more general cuts and abrasions. Thorns or splinters must have been particularly common in days of more widespread manual labour. They could be removed by the application of a snake skin, but for more general flesh wounds the flick from a pig, mixed with the flowers of the elder, should be applied as an ointment. Bleeding must have been a serious problem, when suitable remedies were not available. Apart from the more obvious application of friar's balsam it is traditionally arrested by the application of a spider's web. The cure has given us a story that was first told to me by Ruth Tongue in 1968. It concerns the Monmouth Rebellion, but the location is uncertain:

There was a Manor house very near the church. The Lord went off and left his lady very near her time, on the occasion of the Monmouth Rebellion. She was very worried, and went into the church to speak to the Sexton. While she was there the Lord returned, very badly wounded, his horse exhausted, and his bandages seeping blood. He collapsed on the Parish Chest. At once the Sexton heaved up the lid, and dropped the man inside. The lady sat on the top, spreading her gown to hide all the blood. The Sexton walked up the aisle, treading in any blood to hide it. The soldiers in pursuit were by this time at the church door, but were stopped by the Sexton, who told of his hurry and the labour of the lady. The soldiers were of course too ashamed to go into the church and search. Though they found a dead horse in the orchard they found no sign of the Squire. They went away. The Sexton went back to find the 'dead' Squire in the chest. However he was not dead but alive, as the cobwebs, of which there were a great many in the chest had bound round his wounds and stopped them bleeding.

Treatments for infections of the eyes, ears, nose and throat are next on the list of folk remedies. Toothache was said to be caused by a little white worm in the gum, and cloves were always the traditional remedy. Teething in children required special attention – a silver threepenny piece laid under the pillow. Colds were handled in various ways. Tea could be made from dried flowers from a plant known as Featherful or Featherfew, tiny white blooms which were supposed to be particularly effective for such complaints. Elder blossom tea was also thought to be good. Probably the most well-known cure is rubbing goose fat on the chest – the aroma cleared the nose and banished the germs.

Eye trouble may be treated with juice from the Greater Celandine, so Jack Hurley tells us, since the swallows pluck it for their young who are born blind. Those who lived near Huish cared for similar complaints by bathing with water from a local well which had a good reputation. A sore throat will benefit by wrapping it up at night in a long sock, but this must be unwashed – a remedy that leaves little to the imagination. Coughs are cured by passing through a flock of sheep – whether it was felt that the lanolin would help the cough is not clear, though it is not the only occasion on which these creatures were thought to be prophylactic. There were also remedies for more important illnesses. To strengthen a weak back, rub snails onto the legs, while tonsillitis (quinsy) is cured by eating the creatures raw. If a spider is caught and imprisoned in a box, an attack of fever (ague) would wane along with its life. Stewed rhubarb was always a traditional laxative, and many will remember 'black coated workers' (prunes) from their schooldays, though it is not a treatment limited to this country. The excess caused by over-enthusiastic application of such cures could be arrested by taking meadowsweet, though strictly this was to cure stomach cold and pains in general. With piles we find the perfect folklore charm; they can be avoided by carrying a conker in the trouser pocket. The following anecdote is from about 1970, an example of the continuity of folk cures.

Well, old Bill, he'd had these piles for years – bin to the doctor and all sorts, but it was no good; tried all manner of things, but it was just the same. Of course, we used to take the micky a bit you know, though really it was very painful, so we didn't talk about it too much. Well, one day there was this fellow got an idea about carrying' a conker in your pocket, so old Bill, game for anything he was, said he'd give it a go. Well as it would happen he'd just had a bad do, bin into hospital and everything and left 'cos he was fed up with them doing nothing and just making it worse. Well, he carried the conker in his pocket just like he was told, and tried to forget all about it. Would you believe, after a few days they started to go down, and soon they were all better. Well, he goes to the doctor to show him, and the fellow doesn't believe his eyes – says he looks like he never had piles in his life;
So you can bet your life old Bill won't be caught without his conker now – never on your life.

A fairly well-known traditional cure for hernia, which often occurred in children, involved passing the patient through the split trunk of an ash or elm. They used a particular elm at Huish, in a field called Upper Balls, and kept the split open with wedges. The cure is described in more detail by Mathews.

The idea and the practice is to take the child out in the early morning, when the dew is on the grass. The 'ground ash', that is an ash sapling grown from seed, and never topped, must be split for a length of two or three feet, then prized open, and the child, naked, must be put through the rift from East to West, handed in by a maiden and received by a boy. The split tree is to be bound up again carefully. If it continues to grow, and the split heals over, the child will be cured; if the tree dies, the malady will not be bettered.

Mathews also mentions that hernia could be cured by passing the patient under a blackberry bramble which has re-rooted a distance from the original root.

King's Evil was a general term for scrofula, a morbid constitutional condition with glandular swellings, which may have included tuberculosis and perhaps undiagnosed forms of cancer. It was thought that the condition could be cured by the healing touch of the seventh son of a seventh son. The story told in Somerset is directly linked to the origin of the term King's Evil, based on the belief that a touch from the true monarch would cure the disease. The incident was during Monmouth's visit to Hinton park, presumably during one of the Royal Progresses (1680-2). Elizabeth Parcot, a sufferer from the disease, rushed towards the Duke and tried to touch him. Up till then neither doctors nor any seventh son of a seventh son had been able to help her. Two days after this, she was cured. A folio handbill was circulated 'setting forth the marvellous cure, and a document signed by Henrey Clarke, minister of Crewkerne, two captains, a clergyman and four others lay for some time at the Amsterdam Coffee house, Bartholemew's Lane, London'. The story proved beyond all doubt that Monmouth was not only legitimate, but the true king. It is said that after the Restoration Charles II touched 92,107 people suffering from the disease, thereby validating his claim to the throne. This was another interesting example of a person utilizing traditional beliefs to establish his position in doubtful times. The same source also states that the hand of a hanged felon could be used for this purpose, while Poole records that 'humours' were cured if a dead man's hand was passed overhead nine times. Incidentally, touching a corpse ensured that you would not dream about it.

A child with whooping cough should be taken out early in the morning, preferably when there is a heavy dew, and made to inhale sheep's breath. The same cure is also given by O. Knott in her book *Witches of Wessex*. Her version suggests that the patient should walk through a flock of sheep; but omits the discomforts of the dewy early morning, which might well cause hardship to a severe case.

Not surprisingly cures for rheumatism are very prolific. Some people have great faith in a small copper ring as a charm against stiff joints, and one old remedy from the north of the county suggested a hot drink with plenty of mustard to get the warmth down into them. Either juniper or wild rhubarb cures rheumatism, and bee stings are also supposed to help. Alternatively the painful joint should be struck with a holly branch. Finally, try wrapping yourself in stinging nettles – another traditional cure from the south of the county.

Cramp is treated by binding the skins of eels round the arms, sprains are healed with comfrey, and rickets may be cured by rubbing them with snails – which is similar to the cure for weak backs.

This list must represent a very small proportion of the whole. Some Somerset cures were certainly used from one generation to another, and many were no doubt successful. A few, I am sure, were never of serious value but have been recollected because of their sensational quality. It was without doubt the simple dictum of 'an apple a day' that kept Somerset folk so healthy, even though it was necessary on occasions to take it in liquid form.

9

Illicit Gains

A GROUP OF traditional beliefs and charms offered protection against crime. Many anecdotes describe the exploits of the law-breakers – often with a certain delight in their success, especially when outwitting the officers of law and order. Those simple rhyming verses, sometimes found inside schoolchildren's books were less friendly. Not peculiar to Somerset, they were certainly known in the country during the author's schooldays:

> Black is the raven
> Black is the rook,
> Black is the person
> Who steals this book.

More threatening verses promise severer penalties:

> Steal not this book
> For fear of strife,

For the owner carries
A carving knife.

The ultimate sanction, which clearly belongs to Somerset, runs as follows:

Steal not this book for fear of shame
For here you see the owner's name
And if he catch you by the tail,
He'll clap you into Shepton gaol.

Profane oaths belong to this underworld of folklore, and have a place here. They were a means of establishing one's good faith and once again were often used by school children:

My finger's wet
My finger's dry
God strike me dead
If I tell a lie.

Before reciting this the speaker would wet his forefinger with his tongue, drying it on his clothes before the second line. Finally the forefinger was often drawn across the throat during the final line, as if in a mock suicidal gesture. A simple affirmation could be underscored by saying, with appropriate gestures:

Cross me heart
And cut me throat.

This is no doubt a shorter version of fuller verses quoted elsewhere. It was, in theory at least, believed that if the oath was supporting a false statement instant death or worse would follow. Survival, therefore, proved innocence. The illicit nature of the claim is underlined by the following group of stories centred on the terrible fate of the criminal. Ruth Pierce, a Wiltshire woman, is well remembered in the oral tradition of Bristol. It is said that she withheld 3d. in a business transaction, and died on the spot, but the Bristol version adds that she was turned into a stone, surviving the years in this petrified form. *Aris's Birmingham Gazette* for 12 September 1796 warns:

An awful incident happened lately at Jordan House, near Ilminster. A workman from London, employed on the building there, had paid his addresses to a young woman of the neighbourhood, who, having a suspicion that he was a married man, took an opportunity on Sunday night to question him closely respecting the circumstances; he denied it with oaths, and called for the vengeance of heaven if he was not an unmarried person. However singular it may appear, it is a fact that he had scarce uttered the words when he fell back from the place where they were sitting, and expired almost immediately. He was a very profane wretch, and he left a wife and family.

Presumably the fact that the oath was uttered on a Sunday made it a good deal worse.

Stealing is the most straightforward and widespread means of dishonest acquisition. This story, recorded in Bristol, may have originated in an actual incident.

An old man concealed himself in a dugout in Pie Lane during the day. At night, his companion a goat, issued forth to butt a belated traveller, and whilst thus terror stricken he was robbed.

Sheep-stealing, an arduous and risky activity, provided many stories of times when the poor had to obtain their food as best they could. At its lowest level it developed in the nature of a jibe: 'The last person hanged for sheep-stealing was a Culmstock man, who was also a local preacher.' Culmstock is in Devon, and this tradition marks the strong local antagonism that existed between two border areas. The same outlook is expressed more simply by: 'Never say baa to a Culmstock man. It is reputed that the last man hanged for sheep-stealing was a Culmstock man – and that every other man in the place deserved it too.'

The Blackdowns are particularly rich in stories of this type, some of them still current in oral tradition. A bird, usually an owl or pigeon, sings a warning to the poacher, or alternatively encourages him to commit a more serious crime. Mathews is perhaps the first to record these tales from Somerset. In outline they run as follows;

A sheep-stealer is busy with his thieving, and has just killed a sheep. A wood pigeon in a nearby tree starts cooing, 'Take two, take two'. The sheep-stealer thinks that this is a good idea, and taking another sets off home with the two sheep one on either side of his shoulders. On the way home he stops to rest by a wayside cross. The load slips, and despite the efforts of his boy, who accompanies him, the older man dies from strangulation.

Alternatively:

A sheep-stealer hears a wood pigeon cooing, 'Take two, take two', but before he has time to act on the advice he hears the pigeon for the second time. Now the pigeon sings, 'Rope, rope, hang the man'. The thief thinks again, and goes home.

Perhaps the stories show us that sheep-stealing, like all other forms of poaching, was often simply a deprived section of society taking huge risks for what must have been comparatively small gains. It remained a capital offence until the penal code was reformed in 1832.

The romantic figure of the highwayman sometimes evokes sympathy as, for example, in the case of the legendary Tom Faggus who operated in the Exmoor area, though his exploits can mostly be traced to a literary origin. One writer suggests that the tale was in oral tradition 150 years before the publication of *Lorna Doone* in 1869, and it is in this book that many of the stories can be found. In south Somerset there are still a number of traditions current concerning Windwhistle or the immediate vicinity. It stretches between Chard and Crewkerne, a distance of over seven miles. The busy A.30, which now passes over it, was an old coach route to the south and included a part of the Fosse Way. The stretch of road known as Windwhistle itself was from White Down to St Rayn hill. It rises to a height of about 700 feet, and, being enclosed by an avenue of beech trees, is dark at night. Even today it can seem wild and lonely when the wind screams through the gaunt trees, and the snow drifts in deep ridges across the highway. The deeds of highwaymen, or more simply robbers, in years gone by, probably lie behind many local traditions. The Windwhistle Inn lies about half way along the road, and although the present building is fairly new, it appears that a public house has been on the spot for many years.

The steep combes and isolated villages like Purtington and Chillington would have made ideal places for highwaymen to hide when pursued.

The traditions collected in the area are often quite straightforward:

> Highwaymen used to go up on the main road and rob the stage coaches, as it was a very old road – The Fosse Way, and then they would hide in the caves down over in Chillington and in the woods.

Or, 'People used to say that there were highwaymen up on Windwhistle and that it wasn't safe to travel at night.' The inn itself has particular associations: 'Outside the pub you can see in the wall the rings they used to tie their horses to – it was the highwaymen who used to tie up their horses there.'

The notion of robbers leaving their plunder concealed, never returning due to accident or capture – which meant hanging – explains the widespread tradition in the area about hidden booty, in caves, old wells, or even buried in open ground. Consider the following, given here more or less as it was collected:

> I've been told that there used to be highwaymen about and that they used to do the travellers in and bury them in the wells around this area. The old lady who told me this was about 80, and her parents had lived there all their lives, so she was a good source. She told me that when her father bought the place in 1916 a man had come before from France and asked to dig for treasure, as he believed that there was treasure there. But he refused to allow any such dig. I don't know where the treasure is supposed to be buried; there were no stories about what the treasure was supposed to be – but it could well be something that the highwaymen left. It was true that all round the place there are wells.

Recollections about bodies found in fields are also linked to highwaymen, as in the following account collected from Chillington:

> The highwaymen, when they had killed someone, they would

throw the body into a corn field, and when they cut the corn they would find the body. This happened after they had robbed him. The field was up on the Fosse Way. This was by North Lodge.

Sedgemoor has its own highwayman, though we know as little about his historical existence as we do about Faggus. Here is his story:

Tom Pocock was a highwayman in the seventeenth or eighteenth century. He was particularly successful because when he had robbed a stage coach, or held up a lonely traveller he would ride off at great speed and knew of a rhine which was empty except for a few inches of water. Here he was safe, both from the hounds, who could not follow his scent, and from sight since he was well out of view.

However one day he made a fatal mistake. He told someone of his hiding place, and they were not to be trusted. The next hold up saw him heading to his retreat as usual. He waited in the rhine, hoping his pursuers would pass by. However the next moment he was engulfed in swirling water. At the head of the rhine the sluice gates had been opened, and he drowned in the flooding waters. But his ghost still haunts the rhine to this day.

Smuggling was at its height in the 1730s and was in part due to the heavy import tax, which meant it was only necessary to run one cargo out of three to make a profit. Figures in fact show that smugglers did much better than that. They landed, for example, about 2,000 hogsheads of spirits annually on the coasts of Hampshire, Dorset and Devon, and it took customs officers nine years to capture as many. Oral tradition whitewashes many of these activities but, as with so much illegal behaviour, the result was frequently bloodshed or even the death of innocent parties. Somerset served as a route and disposal centre; the Bristol Channel coast was also probably used and Bristol itself would have provided a ready market. Routes across the southern parts of the county started from, for instance, Lyme Regis, Beer and Seaton, continuing through Axminster, and thence north across the Blackdown Hills to the population centres in the Vale of Taunton. Dorset contraband entered the county via Crewkerne, passing across Windwhistle to either Chard or Ilminster – and so to convenient markets. While smuggling in Somerset never seems to have achieved the structured form that it did elsewhere, folklore quite explicitly links it with both Windwhistle and the Blackdowns.

Tradition refers to ill-gotten gains abandoned in hidden places, the lucky finder reaping the reward of someone else's efforts. One writer describes how the caves and hollows of the Blackdown Hills were used as safe hiding places for goods, which would later be taken to Taunton and sold. The next story from oral tradition also provides the name of a small bridge;

> I heard tell that the smugglers used to come across the Blackdowns, and then down through Bickenhall, passing this house. The bridge on the way to Capland was called Brandy Bridge, and this dates from that time. The goods were sold down in Taunton.

There are tales of contraband concealed in some of the houses at Dowlish Wake, and Allerford was supposed to have had its own smugglers, as the whole village knew. Goods were carried by cart over the old packhorse bridge, and then with, some effort no doubt, up the hill to the hiding places in the woods. Since the whole of Allerford benefited from the smuggling, all kept quiet about what they heard at night.

Not all villages were so cooperative, however, and smugglers sometimes had to invent stories to frighten locals into silence. At Hinton St George a story was put about that on certain nights a phantom coach would be heard (and no doubt seen), and that it was bad fortune indeed to catch a glimpse of it. The smugglers thus made sure of being undisturbed during their nocturnal activities.

Smugglers on Windwhistle have left behind their own tradition, which remains strong in the minds of locals at the small villages in the area. It concerns an incident involving excise men and smugglers, that ended in bloodshed and murder. The stories still told describe ghostly encounters with the spirits of this chase. They are brief and of a general nature:

The spooks come up from Purtington to Windwhistle. They are

horsemen, smugglers, moonrakers. They came across from Cricket St Thomas and across the fields to Purtington, then up to Windwhistle and along the Fosse Way.

Or more simply still, 'When there is a full moon on the right hand side of the road you can hear a horse galloping.' These, and other stories collected at the same time have a number of points in common. They include the sounds of horses or riders, and often mention smugglers or sometimes highwaymen. It seems that they are the remnants of a much longer ghost story, current around the turn of the century. Miss Tongue gave me the following story in 1969:

A man was walking at night on Windwhistle and he heard shouting and galloping. Then a riding officer went by him very badly wounded. Behind him came a smuggler, bent on killing him. Down below in the valley close to the farm were men fighting. The man was frightened and he took to his heels and ran down to the farm for protection. The farmer however took no notice as they were used to hearing the noise.

Miss Tongue records the story in her book *Somerset Folklore* but includes fewer details. The definitive version is to be found in Munford's *Ghosts and Legends of South Somerset*. Here the event is connected with the days of George II and involves a chase across Windwhistle between a smuggler and coastguard. It took place on a very snowy night, and the fight was in the valley of Combe Farm.

Smugglers provide good material for folklore since their activities were usually of the 'rob the rich to feed the poor' variety. The Windwhistle tradition is a timely reminder that freebooting tended to become a somewhat bloody affair.

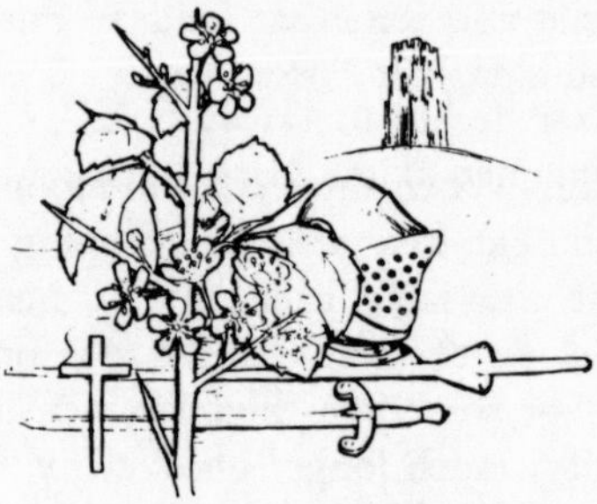

10

History as They Saw it

POPULAR HISTORY has linked Somerset with a number of historical or quasi-historical persons. The interest usually centres on a place or a group of associated localities. Thus Cadbury Camp is linked with King Arthur, and a cavern from which Arthur and his knights will ride out one day is said to be located at the lesser known Cadbury hill near Nailsea. Glastonbury in particular is popularly supposed to be Avalon, though both literary and historical evidence lack the proof some would demand. The origins of the arguments in favour have been discussed elsewhere. Here we shall only consider history as viewed by the folk, which resulted either from hearsay, from the interpretation of events, or from a story that great, great grandmother read to them one evening as a child.

The story of Glastonbury begins with Joseph of Arimathea and the Holy Grail. The complex interaction between literature, history and oral tradition has produced a widely-known corpus of belief, which still carries some weight. Joseph is said to have arrived on English shores at a place now called Wirral: 'Now we are weary all', he is reputed to have said on arrival, and so, according to proper etymology, that place received its name. He then thrust his staff into the ground, and it took root and flourished. It was at Glastonbury Tor that he hid the Holy Grail and he built the first chapel there — forerunner of the Glastonbury Abbey. Arthur Mee has this to say;

It has been in the dreams of men from the days of King Arthur till now, and there are those who will always believe that the Glastonbury Thorn is.the child of one planted by the man who buried Jesus, Joseph of Arimathea. Some say he was sent to bring the good news from Galilee to the Britons, that he thrust his stave into the ground of 'Wirral' Hill where it burst into blossom. It is also said that he buried the Holy Grail at Glastonbury Tor, and built a chapel of wattle and daub which grew through the centuries into the noble Norman abbey which stands magnificent even in ruin to this day.

So the traditions associated with Glastonbury came to centre on the holy thorn and produce a number of incidents which survive in folk belief. The thorn was supposed to bloom on Christmas Day, and this naturally was taken as a sign of its supernatural connections. Needless to say the calendar change of 1752 upset things. *The Gentlemen's Magazine* for January 1753 tells how the inhabitants of Glastonbury had waited for the thorn to bloom on 25 December 1752. Of course nothing happened, but those who knew better were patient until 5 January, the real Christmas day, when the thorn bloomed as usual. There are also stories about those who wished the tree harm, and tried to cut it down. Usually the puritans are blamed; in one case the axe cut the man's leg and chips flew into his eyes. However the tree not only survived, but fathered various descendants which grew from cuttings either taken or sold. As a result holy thorns are supposed to exist at Ilminster, Chaffcombe, Nimmer, Dillington Park, Whitestaunton, West Buckland and Bath. According to some versions the original tree grew from a thorn taken out of the Crown worn by Our Lord.

The thorn was not the only miraculous tree at Glastonbury. Early writers describe a holy walnut which budded on St Barnabas' day (11 June), and never before. Apparently it was cut down by the

Flemmings. There is the same tradition that it sprang from Joseph's staff and it seems that until the destruction of this tree, both were held in similar awe. In a *Life of St Joseph,* printed by Richard Pynson in 1530, we have the following account:

> Great mervaylles men may see at Glastenbury.
> One of a walnut tree that there dooth stande
> In a holy grounde called the semetery
> Harde by the place where Kynge Arthur was founde
> South fro Joseph's chapell it is walled in rounde . . .
> Three hawthornes also that groweth in Werall
> Do burge and bere grene leaves at Christmas
> As fresh as other in May, when the nightyngals
> Wrestes out her notes musycall as pure as glas.

According to Hutton, the thorn – though presumably not the one used to generate the tree – is still preserved in the Nunnery of Stanbrook in Worcestershire. Joseph hid the Grail beneath Chalice Hill, which Hutton explains as slightly towards the left before taking the footpath for the Tor, leaving the Abbey Barn on the right. A variant states that two measures of Christ's blood were buried under the same hill, while the Grail itself is under the tower on the Tor. Two springs flow from the foot of Chalice Hill, and it was believed that these were mixed with Christ's blood. Hutton adds; 'It is impossible to say where this belief arose, though some assert that it was in the ignorance and superstition that followed the Suppression, and that it was not older than the change of religion.' However, in 1750 the locals suddenly decided that the waters had miraculous properties, could heal the sick, and were particularly good for asthma. On 5 May 1751 some 10,000 people gathered from all over the county to drink them.

Today the thorn remains in the Abbey grounds, and blooms regularly at the turn of the year. You can take a distant look through the iron gates, or inspect it closely by paying a sum of money to the ticket collector.

Arthur was said to be descended from Joseph, so to find him associated with Glastonbury is no surprise. The major incident quoted in favour of this was the reported excavation in Henry II 's reign of a coffin inscribed with the well-known:

Hic jacet Arthurus, Rex quondam
Rexque futurus.

The skeleton was huge, the coffin made of oak. Bett however gives
the inscription as;

Hic jacet sepultus inclytus Rex
Arthurus in insula Avonia.

Nearby were found the remains of the Queen, whose yellow hair
was perfectly preserved. However, as a monk grasped it, it fell to
dust. Giraldus Cambrensis, the Chronicler, gives us these details,
and he was present at the excavation. The dig took place in 1190,
and evidently the results were part of both oral tradition and
literature. The inscription at Glastonbury today reads:

The site of King Arthur's Tomb

In the year 1191 the bodies of King Arthur and
his queen were said to have been found on the south
side of the Lady Chapel.
   On 19 April 1278 their remains were removed
in the presence of King Edward 1 and Queen Eleanor
to a black marble.tomb on this site. This tomb
survived until the dissolution of the Abbey in 1539.

Arthur's associations with Somerset do not end with Glastonbury.
Cadbury Castle was said to be Camelot, a notion first put about by
Leland.

At the very South Ende of the Church of South Cadbyri
standithe Camalotte, sumtyme a famose Town or Castelle. . . .
Much Gold Sylver, and Coper of the Romaine Coynes hath been
found ther yn plowing; and lykewise in the felds in the rootes of
this Hille, with many other antique Things and especial byEste.
Ther was found in *hominum memoria* a Horse Shoe of Sylver at
Camallotte. The people can tell nothing ther, but they have herd
say that Arture much resorted to Camalat.

Arthur still appears on Hunting Causeway, and if you are lucky you may see the flash of a silver horse shoe as he rides with his knights to Glastonbury.

Somerset also has a number of place-names linked with Arthur. Near Castle Carry is Arthur's Bridge, and Cadbury has Arthur's Palace and Arthur's Well. Despite the slender historical evidence, Arthur remains a beloved character in Somerset folklore and a salient portion of the Glastonbury legend. The popularity and literary emphasis suggest that people may have been fooled over Arthur and Avalon, though it could be argued that the potential for exploitation must have existed before the success of the geographical Arthur was apparent. But then his spirit is an integral part of Somerset folklore, and was before Leland, Giraldus Gambrensis or even Henry II himself. It is the unhappy linking of legend, place and aspiration that is questioned. Let Arthur Mee's, *The King's England* have the final word:

> The pity is that this shrine of so much that is woven into our island story has been in the keeping of those who have betrayed their trust, and Glastonbury, Isle of Avalon, has become a town of mean streets and commonplace houses, its jewels mixed with vulgar things. Its Tor draws the traveller for many miles round and we all come here on pilgrimage, but having seen what we came to see we hasten away.

King Alfred's association with the county is perhaps less well known, though the most popular story appears in many elementary history books. For this we must thank an early writer called Asser, who wrote a *Life of Alfred*. The work, originally in Latin, was translated by Dr Giles, which accounts for the two variants which appear below. Both Poole and Boger use Asser as their source. Whether the tale was in oral tradition before his time it is impossible to say. At all events, Athelney is now the place where Alfred burnt the cakes. The story runs something as follows;

> King Alfred had been defeated by the Danes, and had fled to the safety of Athelney. This place, where the Tone and Parrett meet, was an area of high land surrounded by water and marsh, inaccessible except by boat. He was therefore comparatively safe

from his enemies.

One day Alfred was sitting near the fire, preparing his weapons. Some small loaves which the cowherd's wife was busy baking started to burn. The hostess being somewhat forthright was not afraid to speak her mind to the King, whom she obviously held responsible for the cakes. Snatching the burnt bread from the hearth she coarsely shouted:

> 'Urere quos cernis panes, gyare moraris
> Cum nimium gaudes hos manducare calentes'

Or perhaps more realistically:

> 'Ca'sn thee mind the ke-aks, man; an'
> dossen zee 'em burn?
> I'm bound thee's eat 'em vast enough
> az zoon az tiz the turn.'

Whatever she really said the incident was commemorated on a plaque erected by John Slade, Lord of the Manor of North Petherton in 1801, dating the event as 879, and adding that, having regained his throne, Alfred in gratitude to Athelney built a monastery, endowed with the surrounding lands.

Muchelney Abbey was founded by Athelstan, King of the West Saxons in 939, though some say it was King Ina who did so. It is generally believed that the abbey owes its origin to Athelstan's victory at Brunanburgh in 937, for which it was a thank-offering, but legend makes it into a penance, for the death of his half-brother Edwin. The King became uneasy when his cup-bearer suggested that his brother was not to be trusted and eventually he cast him adrift in a small boat, with an attendant. Edwin in despair threw himself overboard and drowned. The attendant, who stayed with the boat, was washed ashore, landed in France, and told his story to the French king. Meanwhile Athelstan had second thoughts, and began to doubt his cup-bearer's integrity. The man was finally put to death, and, in penance for allowing himself to be deceived, the King lived in a cell near Langport for seven years. Afterwards he founded the abbey at Muchelney – though much good it did for Edwin.

St Michael's Hill, Montecute is linked to another religious building, this time many miles away at Waltham in Essex. In the days of King Canute, Tofig was Lord of Montecute, then known as Leodgaresburgh, and he was a Dane. A local smith, who was also the sexton, dreamed that Christ appeared to him, instructing him to get some men and go to the priest. He was then to dig at the top of St Michael's Hill. The first time he ignored all this, but the dream recurred, and on the third occasion he was frightened and obeyed. The men dug as directed and found a huge stone. Suddenly it broke in two, and in the cleft they saw a great crucifix of shining black flint, with beneath it a smaller one in wood. There was an old bell and an ancient volume.

When Tofig heard about this he hurried to the spot, put the larger crucifix onto a wain cart, and harnessed to it twelve red oxen and twelve white cows. Accounts now vary as to what happened. Hutton says that he allowed the animals to go as they pleased, and they made straight for Waltham in Essex; no-one could stop them. They halted in front of a cottage which he had used for hunting, so he built an abbey on the spot, and placed the great cross of Leodgaresburgh above the altar. Boger tells a slightly different story. There was opposition from the people of Montecute, who did not want the cross moved from their own village. Moreover the oxen would not budge, as they obviously sided with the locals. Tofig named all the shrines as an incentive to the animals, but this had no effect. Finally he hit on Waltham, and they then set off quite happily.

There is a story that Harold kneeled before the cross prior to the Battle of Hastings, and it bowed to him, so the English in the Battle shouted, 'Holy Cross, Holy Cross'. Harold was also buried at this place. Once again it is impossible to say how much derived originally from oral tradition, and how much from literary sources. It is certain that ecclesiastical institutions often tried to enhance their reputation by perpetuating 'miraculous' stories of their own origins, a trait that is of course not limited to the Church. In this case both sources quoted obtained their material from the same authority, with some additional material, but it is not clear from whom they learnt the story of Leodgaresburgh and Tofig's holy rood.

Thomas à Becket's place in Somerset folklore rests rather with his assassins and I am indebted to Mr. J. Hurley for the following information which appears in his book, *Legends of Exmoor*. The church at Sampford Brett is said to have been built by one of the murderers de Brito, in atonement, and Williton church was founded for the same reason by Fitzurse. Folklore has buried two of the murderers on Flat Holm, and one of them, William de Tracey, moans to this day as he leaves to do his penance at Woolacombe. There he must make bundles of sand, and bind them together with string of the same substance. His groaning is the fog horn on Flat Holm.

Legend has given to two of the four knights whose crime caused them to be execrated by all men, graves on Flat Holm. There is not a shred of evidence in support, but it would be a sorry day for legend and would make this book superfluous, if evidence there was!

Flat Holm, sprawling in the grey waters of the Channel's shipping lane, has been considered a fit place for the graves of men whose hands bore the stain of unpardonable crime. Legend has put three of the knights there ... Tracey, Fitzurse and de Brito ... but fact shows only two graves'.

Another curious feature is that the graves were dug north and south instead of the Christian way, east and west ... an inference that those whose feet did not lie towards the morn would not be rising at the Resurrection.

Cardinal Wolsey is another historical character who has found his way into Somerset Folklore. Stories about the Cardinal are still told at Lopen, though in fact it appears that the following incident may have occurred in Ilchester:

They put someone in the stocks at Lopen, but I can't remember who it was, but he was a very important man. It was Lord Paulett who did this.

Cardinal Wolsey came to the village [Lopen] when he was a young man, and everyone gave him cider, which got him into trouble and into the stocks at Lopen, but I've seen the ones at Martock.

Hulbert in his 'Survey of Somerset Fairs' records the story, writing that Wolsey, 'then only a rector at Limington, in the time of Henry VII, got drunk and disorderly, and was consequently clapped in the stocks by the first Sir Amias Paulett of Hinton St George'. When he became Lord Chancellor he got his revenge by ordering Paulett to London and compelling him to stay in the Middle Temple for five or six years. There is no doubt that in 1500 Wolsey was vicar and schoolmaster of Limington, a small village near Ilchester, but just how he came to be associated with Lopen remains a mystery, unless the incident did in fact take place there.

In the reign of Edward III Dunster was ruled by John de Mohun and his wife was Joan.

The tale is that, on receiving a request from the inhabitants of Dunster for certain lands adjacent to the town whereon to depasture their cattle freely and in common, John de Mohun granted his lady, who interceded on the townspeople's behalf, as much land as she could go round barefoot in one day, which land she might afterwards bestow on her dependants.

The same story is given by Fuller in *Fuller's Worthies*:

She obtained from her husband so much ground for the common of the town of Dunster as she could in one day (believe it a summer one for her ease and advantage) compasse about, going on her naked feet.

The Civil War must have made little impact on Somerset; there are few stories in the county about those troubled years. In any case the preoccupation with Monmouth has tended to dim any recollections of the earlier strife, and folklore has blurred the two events. Thus Barrington Hill near Broadway is said to have a Fight Ground where Cromwell's troops engaged in battle. In fact it was the site of a small skirmish during Monmouth's time. A nearby lane, known as 'Oliver's Lane', is either the cause or the result of the confusion. At Broadway one informant said that the tree in the vicarage garden was a 'Cromwell Tree', that is one under which Cromwell rested or addressed his men. The same was occasionally said of the sweet chestnut at Whitelackington, but history associates it with Monmouth.

However there was a battle at Langport in July 1645, and local tradition has made the mounds in Sheepslade into graves of soldiers who fell there. It is also said that skeletons with heavy boots were dug up in a Huish garden, and that these were men who died then. Another account has it that the Roundheads carved their initials in the beams of Pibsbury windmill. Again the depression worn in the stone of the church doorway is where Cromwell sharpened his sword before battle – an interesting piece of folklore, since it is popularly believed that the hollows in the buttress of Weston Zoyland church were made by Monmouth's men sharpening their swords, prior to Sedgemoor.

Monmouth without doubt overshadows all other characters in the county's historical traditions. The incidents in the story of the unfortunate Duke mostly took place in Somerset, and Sedgemoor where he finally met defeat could hardly be more central. Many good words have been written, sympathy has been expressed and theories suggested. But to the ordinary person two points stand out that make the Monmouth affair of particular importance. The first was that the rebellion involved either to a greater or lesser extent a vast section of the population in the areas concerned, and second the reprisals at the Bloody Assize not only alarmed and endangered a large number of people, but were so traumatic that hatred of the unjust Judge Jeffreys lives on to this day.

Monmouth first arrived in the county in 1680, during one of his semi-royal progresses. These appear to have been an attempt to gain favour with the people – but his motives are irrelevant to the folk traditions that formed around his memory. Monmouth certainly went to Whitelackington, Barrington Court, Forde Abbey, Chard, Ilminster, and perhaps Hinton St George. Most of the remaining folklore describes how he visited various places, and interestingly this is commonly said to be prior to the Battle of Sedgemoor – an impossible chronology. This same confusion is a feature of the traditions dealing both with Monmouth and Judge Jeffreys. In fact Monmouth came to Somerset in 1685, after landing at Lyme Regis on 11 June. He arrived at Ilminster on 17 June and from there proceeded to Taunton where he collected additional forces, and marched out to the battle of Sedgemoor, which was fought on 6

July 1685. He was in the area a little less than four weeks.
Tradition tells it rather differently. (In each of the following
examples the name of the place concerned appears in italics.)

The old house here is called Knight's House. This name comes
from the field on which the house was built which is called
Knight's Field. The story of the name is that the knights
assembled there before the battle of Sedgemoor. A metal
ornamental knight was dug up in the garden, which could have
been from a helmet. This is now a door knocker.   *Broadway*

There was once a castle up there, and the old part of the farm
house which is now made into the kitchen was formerly the
stables of the Castle. Wellington or Monmouth hid in the
house.   *Castle Neroche*

In the churchyard field are the remains of an old house now used
as a barn, and it is commonly reported that the Duke of
Monmouth slept here the night before his defeat at the battle of
Sedgemoor.   *Catcott, from C. H. Poole*

At the old inn, Monmouth is supposed to have stayed on 26 June
1685 in his march from Glastonbury to Keynsham before the
Battle of Sedgemoor. While at the inn, a man hoping for the
reward offered for the Duke tried to shoot him, but according to
a ballad the Duke;
              Gently turned him round
              And said, 'My man, You've missed your mark
              And lost your thousand pound'.'
                          Norton St Philip. from E. Hutton

Monmouth certainly did not visit Norton St Philip on the date
suggested, though it is possible that he passed through in 1680.
      The association with Whitelackington is still a significant feature
in local folk tradition. It is often said that Monmouth's visit took
place after the battle, and he is usually a fugitive. He hid in the
house, and there was a rope with which he hanged himself. Others
say that he hid in the oak tree in the grounds. The tree was in fact a
sweet chestnut, blown down in 1897.

Whitelackington also appears in traditions in a different context, for one of the three sons of the Speke family – the current owner – was hanged in public in Ilminster market place. It appears that George, the father, was sympathetic to Monmouth, and had entertained him in 1680. One of the sons, John, actually took part in the rebellion, but escaped and travelled abroad until the Restoration. Hugh, a political activist, was already in prison; he was found guilty of sedition following the publication of a pamphlet. Charles, the third son, is said to have shaken hands with Monmouth as he passed through Ilminster in 1685, and it was he who was hanged there following the Bloody Assize. His death was partly to replace John, who 'could not be found. The incident has left behind it a body of tradition;

One of the Spekes was hanged for shaking hands with Monmouth when he came through Ilminster, since he knew him. He was of course sentenced by Judge Jeffreys. His brother avoided being hanged by escaping.   *Moolham*

Another version collected from Dowlish Wake told how one of the Spekes was hanged for refusing to fight, preferring instead to stay at home with his lady. He, poor fellow, met his end on Toller Down.

The Battle of Sedgemoor was fought on the moors a short distance from Weston Zoyland. The church there was used by Monmouth's troops before the battle, and as we have seen he was said to be responsible for the hollow grooves in the buttress of the building. Many of the troops saw it again after the battle, brought there as prisoners. There is a tradition recorded by Poole to the effect that Richard Alford, the churchwarden in 1685, supported Monmouth. He saved himself from execution during a subsequent visit of James II by offering the soldiers a jug of cider embossed with the King's head. In this way he avoided any awkward questions. The battle itself was fought early in the morning of 6 July. The result was something of a foregone conclusion, since Monmouth's troops were ill-equipped and poorly trained. It is said that the action was precipitated by one of his men slipping into a rhine and firing his pistol by mistake, thus alerting the King's forces. Whether this incident made much difference to the final result is very doubtful, but there was a tradition that a gipsy had warned Monmouth to beware of the 'Rhine'. He naturally believed that this meant the German River, and gave it no thought when he was in Somerset.

Judge Jeffreys was sent to sort out the rebels, and, by the horrid example of a few, ensure that the same thing did not recur. He started his journey from Winchester, and visited Salisbury, Dorchester, Exeter, Taunton, Bristol, before leaving for Wells on 21 September. Thus, only a few weeks after the rebellion, those judged guilty had been punished, and, by the end of September, most major centres in the region had been visited. Courts were held in the larger towns, though hangings took place locally. Once again, oral tradition tends to view events in a different light. It describes Jeffreys visiting all sorts of places to which in fact he never went.

Judge Jeffreys lived at Ilford Bridges Farm, and there was talk that there was hanging there.   *Puckington*

Judge Jeffreys used to live at Crickleaze.   *Combe St Nicholas*

Swell Court was so called because this was one of the many places where Judge Jeffreys held his assize. He was not at all bothered who he put to death. Other big houses further away are called Manors, because he did not have a court there.   *Ludney*

There is a preservation order on the old nail studded door on the Market Square side of the now closed Swan Inn in Ditton Street, Ilminster. This is because Judge Jeffreys passed through this doorway on his way to the Assizes in Ilminster.   *Horton*

The cruel punishments inflicted, which included quartering, have left a strong impression on local memory, and Jeffreys is still regarded as a villain. These traditions however are limited to sites where people are said to have been hanged:

There were three men hanged on Herne Hill after the Monmouth rebellion. There were also three hanged in the Square at Ilminster, and three on the Beacon.   *Horton*

Ruth Tongue tells an interesting story about a farmer near Street, whose son was put to death by the Judge. The farmer sought revenge by using sympathetic magic against his enemy. This illustrates the strength of local feeling.

For some reason Jeffreys has also become associated with the village of Stocklinch, and it is popularly supposed that he was brought back there after his death. In fact he died and was buried in London. Stories vary, from the statement that Jeffreys was buried in the vault of the church, to more detailed traditions telling of his return, by night, to die, or describing his headless body brought back for burial in a coffin shorter than the others in the vault. It is a macabre ending to a period in history that has contributed as much to Somerset legend as any other single incident.

Not all traditions of past occurrences have famous or important people as their main characters. From time to time events take place involving quite ordinary people, and these pass into the body of belief. But they have to be significant in their narrative content, and the actions are usually limited to miraculous happenings or serious crimes. Since the folklore of miracles belongs to the same realm as that of the saints, it is crimes like murder that pass into popular history. In Chapter 6 we saw how crossroad killings and burials create ghost stories. More commonplace murders are also absorbed into tradition, in ways that usually differ to a greater or lesser extent from the actual facts. A case in point was the murder of Samuel Churchill at Knowle St Giles in 1879. He was killed by his wife, and she was hanged for the crime a short while afterwards at Taunton. This is often recounted locally, and many of the details remain intact. But names are altered or changed, the circumstances of the crime are modified, and ghosts are supplied where necessary. Murder is remembered because it is worth remembering, and it passes into folklore to be transmuted and adapted in fulfilling the function of all historical legend; an indication of the feelings of the time, rather than an account of the incidents that gave rise to them.

—11—

Entertainment
and Humour

THERE WAS always time for relaxation. Folklore records the manners of the period and much of what follows in this chapter is an expression of how people enjoyed themselves before the days of radio, television and mass media. There were public entertainments, and through them it was possible for material to be disseminated more rapidly and widely than personal or private traditions ever could be. Hence the more celebrated expressions and rhymes will not be peculiar to Somerset though many such have been recorded in the county.

Sports were often of a seasonal nature. While fox hunting required equipment within the financial reach of comparatively few, beagling was available to anyone with a strong pair of legs. Rough shooting was also a winter pastime. Rabbits were the favourite game, as strict laws protected pheasants and the other birds traditionally associated with the upper classes. Duck-shooting was always popular on Sedgemoor in the winter months when the moors were flooded. Flat-bottomed punts were used and on these the huge duck gun was mounted – about six to eight feet in length, and taking over a pound of shot. These guns are now gone, but sportsmen still shoot the duck, and still occasionally get a soaking with an upturned boat or an unsteady footing. The competitive sports on dry land were often wrestling, cudgels, and fair time pastimes – like chasing a greasy-tailed pig and climbing for a ham, this last in Huish at Eastertide. Horse races and the Donkey Derby continue to this day.

One game that has failed to survive is fives. This is a ball game played with the hands, or a bat, against a wall or walls. In Somerset it seems that hands were used and only one wall was required. Since it had to be of some height, and cost money, the church tower sometimes served this purpose, usually to the irritation of the authorities. Fives was once a genuinely popular game, and the reason for its disappearance has never been satisfactorily explained.

There are altogether ten recorded fives walls, or adapted walls. Of these, five are still standing, and were built specifically for the purpose; a sixth, at Ilminster, was partially demolished during a storm at the end of the last century. It was then used to build the swimming pool at the local Boys' Grammar School and the initialled stones, some of them upside down, were clearly visible on the low wall supporting the side. The remaining four walls utilized church towers, or in one case the end of some cottages. It was the use of church towers that apparently caused some trouble. There was a very tall poplar tree by the tower of West Buckland church. It was cut down because it became unsafe, but the original reason for its planting, along with another, was to prevent fives being played as the game was causing damage to the churchyard, and desecration of the graves. One of the trees died before it reached maturity, but the second did its job well. Local tradition does not explain how the trees survived their infancy. At Martock there are said to be a number of small notches used for scoring, and hand and foot holes used to climb onto the roof to retrieve the ball. Here, too, the game was finally banned. Players at Montecute removed decorative carved masonry from the side of the tower to improve the playing area. The vicar greatly annoyed, had a stone market cross erected in the middle of the court, and this effectively stopped the game. The base of the cross can still be seen, and one side of the tower shows signs of mutilation.

Mumming also provided entertainment, and generally took place around Christmas time, especially on Christmas Eve. It seems to have been fairly general throughout the county, and was certainly well established at the beginning of the century in the Stone Easton, Kilmersdon, Frome and Castle Cary areas. Ruth Tongue describes the Crowcombe Mummers about the same period. They enacted a simple story with King George, who usually kills the Turkish Knight, the King of Egypt or another villain. He was often responsible for the death of a second, perhaps comic figure, and the fights provided a moment of high drama. A Doctor appeared at the end to restore life to the dead and the play concludes with an appeal for money or food made by the chief coordinator and organiser, who is usually Father Christmas. Female characters were not unknown.

The mummers' plays have been variously interpreted as the triumph of good over evil, or the rebirth of the spring at the turn of the year. Whatever the origins of the custom, it was performed as a local activity of considerable importance belonging essentially to a specific holiday season. The appeal of the mummers clearly rested upon the kindly reception they would receive from friends, and the humour of anything so unpretentiously amateur. They visited a number of houses on Christmas Eve, performed their play, and walked on to their next venue. C. H. Poole gives a more precise description with some variation of detail:

> Mumming ... consists of persons concealing their appearance and performing a drama which embodies the time-honoured legend of St George and the Dragon, with many whimsical adjuncts, winding up with appeals for money, couched in rude verse.

Stories are not widely favoured in popular humour, but it seems that village entertainment created oral traditions that may have originally come from literary sources – books of collected music-hall songs and other material. Some examples of this kind were collected from Drayton. Tellers are few, since the material requires careful handling and a captive audience.

There was a young man called Jan who went to church every

Sunday evening. After church he would hold hands with Mary Jane and say goodnight. After a while he decided to be a bit daring and hold on to her hand a little bit longer. So one Sunday he didn't let go of her hand and said, 'Why can't we be in love? Our horses plough in the same meadows, our ducks swim in the same pond and our cats sing a duet on the same roof. Why can't we be in love? I can feel my heart fluttering inside me waistcoat and me chest heaving inside me shirt.'

They walked down the lane together and they stood by the stile. He hugged her a bit and the old stile gave way and she fell flat on her back and fainted.

He thought to himself, 'Brandy's good for bringing people round', so he went into the house and poured out a drop of brandy. He took the brandy and went back to the stile to see if she had come round. As she had not he went back and poured himself a bigger brandy, and went to the stile. She was just beginning to come round because he could see her eyes fluttering.

By this time her mother and some of the congregation had arrived. He felt a bit merry and started to dance with her mother. Her mother said 'Don't talk to Mary Jane again, or see her again'. And he replied, 'I don't want to, if it takes half a bottle of brandy to bring her round.'

This is a good example of Somerset humour. Here is a second story, from the same source.

One Sunday morning a young man went to visit Mary, a maid at the vicarage. He said, 'Cor Mary, something smells good in here, what's the vicar got for dinner?'

She replied, 'Sheep's head and five dumplings.'

He suggested a game of hide and seek, so she went off to hide, and he took one of the dumplings out of the pot. He did this four times, so there was only one dumpling left. He said, 'I'd better go now, the vicar will be back soon.'

But before he went he gave the sheep's head and dumpling in the pot a good stir with a ladle. The vicar came in and said 'What's for dinner Mary?' She said 'Sheep's head and dumplings' and she took off the lid to show him and said 'Quick Vicar, the sheep's head has eaten four dumplings and is chasing the other one like mad.'

Sometimes the joke depends more specifically on the ignorance or stupidity of the main character. This is a well-known motif particularly in the countryside where, for some reason, the gullibility of the bumpkin causes amusement. The following story collected by R. W. Patten from the Ilminster area illustrates the continuity of traditional humour:

> An old farmer came into some money so he bought a Rolls-Royce. It was delivered in due course and, try as he would, he could not start it. So he sent for a mechanic who pointed out that the car was started, but was so quiet that he could not hear it.

Cats figure more than once in droll stories and rhymes from Somerset. They share a common theme in that the creatures are not only a law unto themselves, but need treating with particular care. The following is again from Drayton;

> Now since the cat married the cat
> That lives next door to us
> They stay out all the night
> And howl with all their might.
> Oh yesterday morning I collared them both
> Their games I meant to check
> I decorated the pair of them
> With a brick right round the neck.
> I popped them into the cistern
> But this morning when I awoke
> They both sat on the windowsill
> And they began to croak,
> 'Here we are again
> Here we are again'.
> I got up and gave a shout
> 'How the devil did you get out?'
> Both of them said 'Miaow'
> And bawled with might and main
> 'We drank the water and ate the bricks
> So here we are again'.

It is possible that the last line leads into a song. The next example is from Horton:

> Not last night, but the night before
> Two Tom cats came knocking at my door.
> I went down to let them in
> And they knocked me down with a rolling pin.
> The rolling pin was made of brass
> They lifted me up and tanned my arse.

The story of the man who loses himself unaccountably in the woods at night is popular. Here is one version:

Jacob Stone got lost going home one night, and got very frightened. An owl in a tree goes 'Who who', and Jacob thinks that he's asking him.
 'Jacob Stone zur.'
 'Who who, whoooo?'
 'Jacob Stone zur, tailor and honest a man as lived.'
 'Weet, weet, wait.'
So he waited, scared to death until his friend came along and heard him talking and took him home. Everyone thought it was a huge joke.

Local rhymes are humourous or even mildly slanderous. From Frome comes:

> Rode fete, Beckington rout
> The devil's in Frome and they can't get him out.

One informant was asked about traditions of the devil:

Do you think the devil's still here somewhere?
Oh yes, I reckon you'll find the old fellow down in the village in one or two places.

The small hamlets on Exmoor have their own rhymes;

> Oare, Culbone, and Stoke Pero
> Are three such places as you seldom hear o'.

Jack Hurley collected this, which is similar;

> Culbone, Oare, Stoke Pero
> Parishes three where no parson'll go.

Sometimes bells are said to sing words as they chime, and again they can be humorous:

> Muchelney says, Who can beat we five?
> Langport says, We seven can,
> And the bell of Long Load says, Liar

Riddles are certainly the most exasperating form of wit, frustrating the victim and boosting the ego of the riddler; for unless you know the answer it is unlikely that your reply will be correct. Thus a 'Stand up in the house and talk' is a clock and a broom is a 'Go all round the house and stand up in the corner'. More challenging is:

> What is the difference between a farmer and a dressmaker?
> He gathers what he sows, and she sews what she gathers.

The 'what is the difference between' variety, well-known elsewhere, certainly occurred in the north of the county in the 1950s;

> What is the difference between an elephant and a letter box?
> Don't know.
> I'll never send you to post a letter again.

An umbrella is described with more charm:

> I've got one leg to stand upon
> Plenty of arms have I.
> I have a wrap around me

And I am not always dry
Sometimes narrow,
Sometimes wide
Often you'll find me at your side.

Alternatively the rhyme may contain a concealed name:

As I was going through London Town
I met a London scholar
He shook hands and drew off his hat
I pray you tell me his name
I've told you his name already

(Andrew)

Another version was told in Bristol in the 1950s.

As I walked over London Bridge
I met a man I knew
He took off his hat and drew off his gloves
I pray you tell me his name.

The most subtle of these is the following, also remembered from the north of the county:

There were two people came along the street.
One was the father of the other one's son
What relation were they?

(Husband and wife)

A widespread tradition involves hairs on the palm of the hand. Thus, all honest men have a tuft on the palm of their hands. An alternative version runs;

Do you know what the first sign of madness is?
No.
Hairs on the palms of your hands.
And do you know what the second sign is?
No.
Looking for them.

Nonsense rhymes, like riddles, are not confined to this county, but may exhibit local variation. A common form, popular among children, gives a general meaning developed to the absurd by the demands of the rhyme;

> What's the time
> Half past nine
> Hang your britches
> On the line
> When they're dry
> Bring them in
> Hang them up
> With a safety pin.

Its effect may depend on a degree of implied or stated impropriety. Indeed a list of such rhymes would fill a separate book. Space only permits a few of the more acceptable;

> 'Behave yourself nicely' said father
> 'For manners have long been our boast.'
> 'Manners be buggered' said Charlie
> And did a gert gob on his toast.

Sometimes the obscenity is obvious from the rhyme, and the verse deliberately omits the required word. Replacing it with another makes the meaning clear, while pretending not to give offence;

> Spider, spider on the wall
> Spider, spider, oh so small
> Don't you know the wall's been plastered
> Come down here you silly spider.

A well-known sequence of rhymes uses another technique to avoid impropriety:

> Ask no questions, tell no lies
> Did you ever see a policeman doing up his
> Flies are a nuisance, flies are a pest
> Did you ever see a lady looking down her
> Vesta matches are the best.

Pure nonsense rhymes rely on the total absurdity of what is being said, which in itself is a form of entertainment;

> I took myself to the pictures
> And had a front seat in the back
> I fell from the pit to the gallery
> And broke a front bone in my back.

The Opies believe this second type is probably older;

> One fine day in the middle of the night
> Two dead man got up to fight
> Back to back they faced each other
> Drew their swords and shot each other.

Songs helped to make the tedious hours of work pass more pleasantly. Unfortunately many are now lost, but Mathews has recorded two. The first is a ploughing song, though the tune is not known;

> Broad and Beauty, do your duty
>   Chupader, woah,
> Time and Reason, work for Season
>   Chupader, woah,
> Young and old, work when you're told
>   Chupader, woah.

Bird-scaring was a job usually undertaken by young boys, and he records that they would sing:

> He, hi, ho, here I go, up to my knees in snow,
> Girt bird, little bird, ait enough, pick enough,
> My master got enough
> Home is his barley mow.

Cider has certainly contributed to Somerset tradition. It developed its own stories, jokes and rituals — some, like wassailing, have already been examined in detail. The toast was a prelude to the drink. The following verses collected by R. W. Patten come from Drayton:

Now I've travelled all day
Through mud and clay
I'm like a desert fish
I haven't had a very much to drink today
So I think I'll drink of this.

Did I drink to success
Or did I drink in vain
I didn't drink very much last time
So I think I'll drink again.

Now I've drunk to success
I love a flowing cup
I bain't likely to have any more tonight
So I think I'll drink it up.

'Wassail' itself was of course a toast, wishing good health. The briefest would do for every day, and longer, more elaborate versions were reserved for special occasions;

Good luck to the hoof and the horn
    Good luck to the flock and the fleece
Good luck to the growers of corn
    With the blessings of Plenty and Peace.

The next is less polished and possibly more traditional:

Here's a health to the barley-mow
    Here's a health to the man
    Who very well can
Both harrow and plough and sow.

Some toasts were quite bluntly expressed;

I like to zee 'ee come
I like to zee 'ee go
I like your company,
I don't like yer hours;
Zo I be to home,
An' I wish you all was.

There was a lot of fun at the expense of those who drank too much, and people said of someone normally rather taciturn:

'Aw, he'em like a hedgehog, opens when he's wet.'

Rough cider itself is known as 'Tanglefoot', because of what it does to the feet on the homeward journey, but this little verse contains good advice:

> Beer on cider makes a good rider
> Cider on beer makes you feel queer.

Cider was drunk from a variety of containers. The cider jug, often considerably larger than a pint, was the most popular. In the field a firkin was used. The pots or jugs sometimes had inscriptions which fulfil a similar function to the toasts discussed above. From central Somerset comes the following, noted from a drinking cup:

> Let the wealthy and the great
> Roll in splendour and in state
> I envy them not I declare it.
> I eat my own lamb and my chicken and ham
> I shave my own fleece and wear it
> I have lawns, I have bowers, I have fruit,
> I have flowers
> The lark is my morning alarmer
> So jolly boys, now here's Good speed to the plough
> Long life and success to the farmers.

The owner of this cup was obviously not a farm labourer, though it is interesting that the second verse runs;

> He that by the plough must thrive
> Himself must either
> Hold or Drive;
> God speed the plough.

The following inscription on a two-gallon cider jug, which would have been used to replenish drinker's pots, comes from Porlock;

De Spise me not be Cose I am small. Fill me offen
I will ples you awll. God save the King and Joseph
Rue. Porlock 1738.

My the Honest hart never know no Distriss. 1738.

The 'Yard of Ale', still drunk in Somerset, is a widespread custom.
The vessel is a long cylindrical glass with a bulb at the end and the
drinker must consume the lot in one draught – or at least as quickly
as possible. The shortest time wins. The custom still exists and is
increasing in popularity.

In many respects traditional Somerset lore has survived because
of its infectious humour and power to please. Calendar customs, oral
traditions and casual observances are continued in part at least,
because they make difficult periods less hard to bear, and ease times
of strain. The contribution that so many of them make to life's
pleasures establishes their value in our modern society and no doubt
saves them from condemnation as outmoded, uncivilized and
unintelligent. The function of folklore in social entertainment should
never be overlooked.

Notes

DIRECT reference to a work indicates that it was the source of the material used. *See* implies either a direct alternative reference, or a similar source. *See also* indicates related material or additional comment on the topic under discussion.

1 *Popular Beliefs,* pages 19-34
BOVET : *Pandaemonium or the Devil's Cloyster,* 1684. R. Bovet was a native of Wellington.
FAIRY FAIR : Briggs and Tongue, *Folktales of England,* 1965, p. 37. Also recorded by Miss Tongue in *Somerset Folklore,* 1965, pp. 112-3. The story about the farmer receiving leaves in his change is also recorded in Briggs and Tongue *Folktales of England,* pp. 33-4.
PIXY HOARD : Mathews, F. W. *Tales of the Blackdown Borderland,* 1923, p. 55.
OFFERINGS TO PIXIES : Hurley, J. *Legends of Exmoor,* 1973, p. 32.
FAIRY MIDWIFE : Briggs and Tongue *op. cit.,* pp. 38-9. Mathews *op. cit.,* p. 59.
MINEHEAD MARKET : Hurley *op. cit.,* p. 34.
SEEING FAIRIES : Mathews *op. cit.,* p. 55.
BROADWAY : South Somerset, 1968.. See, Palmer, K. *Oral Folk-tales of Wessex,* pp. 48-9.
DOWLISH WEST : See Palmer *op. cit.,* pp. 46-8. Traditions collected from south Somerset, 1968-9.
UPHILL CHURCH : *English Dance and Song,* Winter, 1971. R. Manville, Weston-Super-Mare.
CRICKET COURT : Oxenford, 1968.

CADBURY CASTLE : Hutton, E. *Highways and Byways in Somerset,* 1912, p. 227. Collected from Rev. J. A. Bennett.

CASTLE NEROCHE : See Palmer *op. cit.,* pp. 151-3. The literary version is in Mathews *op. cit.,* p. 25. Miss Tongue also has a version, *op. cit.,* p. 14. Historically the dig appears to have taken place about 100 years before 1854, as an article by Rev. F. Warre in *Proceedings,* 1854, 5.1, p. 30ff. illustrates. Further digs were made of an archeological nature in 1853, 1903, and 1962.

BROOMFIELD : Hurley, J. *op. cit.,* p. 56.

SIMONS BURROW : The first record of this appears to be in Lackington, J., *Life of Lackington* (13th ed. 1793), pp. 327-8. Mathews records the story, including the crock of gold, *op. cit.,* p. 31. Tongue *op. cit.,* p. 14 mentions the gold also, but is less specific as to its location.

ROBIN HOOD'S BUTTS : Mathews *op. cit.,* p. 99. Tongue *op. cit.,* p. 13.

STAPLE FITZPAINE : Palmer *op. cit.,* p. 151. Collected from Combe St Nicholas, 1969.

CULM DAVY : Mathews *op. cit.,* pp. 100-1.

COCK CROW STONE : Tongue *op. cit.,* p. 12.

CARACTACUS STONE : See Hurley *op. cit.,* pp. 53-4. Miss Tongue records a further legend about the stone, *op. cit.,* p. 12.

HAM STONE : Bett, H. *English Myths and Traditions,* 1952, p. 51. Hutton *op. cit.,* p. 258.

WIMBLESTONE : Tongue *op. cit.,* p. 12.

DIANA : Collected Hinton St George, 1969.

MONKSILVER : Hutton *op. cit.,* p. 325. Hurley also records the tradition and points out that the tools are not only emblems of the passion, but that the window dates from 1845 when the church was restored.

HUISH CHURCH : Wyatt, I. *The Book of Huish,* 1933, p. 25.

CHRISTENING PARTY : Mathews *op. cit.,* pp. 16-7.

CONFIRMATION : Poole, C. H. *The Customs, Superstitions and Legends of the County of Somerset,* (1877, 2nd ed. 1970), p. 30.

WEDDING SONG : Opie, I. & P. *The Lore and Language of School Children,* p. 303, gives the second and less familiar version, recorded from Bath.

WEDDING ROPE : See Wyatt *op. cit.,* p. 95. Tongue *op. cit.,* p. 135.

HUISH : Wyatt, *op. cit.,* p. 95.

MUCHELNEY : Informant, Muchelney, Jan. 1973. Collected R. W. Patten.

CORPSE CURES : Tongue *op. cit.*, p. 136. Poole *op. cit.*, p. 52.

BLEEDING CORPSES : See Palmer *op. cit.*, pp. 49-50, for full details and documentation. Tongue *op. cit.*, p. 101 tells the story about Babb. For Jack White's Gibbet, see Briggs and Tongue, *Folktales of England*, 1965, pp. 96-8. Also Tongue *op. cit.*, p. 104. *The Somerset Year Book*, 1922, pp. 60-3 gives the full details of the event and the story, and is well worth reading by anyone interested in the tradition.

BURIAL FACE DOWN : Tongue *op. cit.*, p. 147.

BROWN'S FOLLY : Collected by R. W. Patten, Drayton, 29.8.71. See Palmer *op. cit.*, p. 96.

HINTON HOUSE : Palmer *op. cit.*, p. 96.

OLIVER KING : see Poole *op. cit.*, p. 72.

2 *Saints and Settlers*, pages 35-43

DUNDRY : Poole, C. H. *The Customs, Superstitions and Legends of the County of Somerset*, 1877, 2nd ed., 1970, p. 76.

BLEADON : Briggs and Tongue, *Folktales of England*, 1965, pp. 80-1.

MALREWARD : Poole, *op. cit.*, pp. 117-8.

SEAVINGTON : Palmer, K. *Oral Folk-tales of Wessex*, 1973, p. 17. Correct etymology from Ekwall, E. *Concise Dictionary of English Place Names*, 1951, under 'Sevenhampton'.

DOWLISH WAKE : S. Somerset, 1968.

SHAVE LANE : Donyatt, 1968.

CARANTOC : Hurley, J. *Legends of Exmoor*, 1973, p. 50. Palmer *op. cit.*, p. 148.

CONGAR : Bett, H. *English Legends*, 1952, p. 53. Poole *op. cit.*, pp. 75-6. Hutton, E. *Highways and Byways in Somerset*, 1912, p. 389. For a further version of St Congar's walking stick see, Tongue, R. L. *Somerset Folklore*, 1965, p. 185.

DECUMAN : The story is well known and is recorded by many writers; Hurley *op. cit.*, p. 50. Poole *op. cit.*, pp. 122-3. The skull on Wells Cathedral is recorded by Hutton *op. cit.*, p. 377.

INDRACTUS : Poole *op. cit.*, pp. 106-7. Capgrave records the pillar of light over the grave. Ruth Tongue records the detail of the ill omen associated with the Shapwick light, *op. cit.*, p. 96.

DUNSTAN : Boger, E. *Myths, Scenes and Worthies of Somerset,* 1887, p. 146. See also Poole *op. cit.,* pp. 88-9, and Hutton *op. cit.,* pp. 158-9.

KEYNA : Bett, H. *op. cit.,* p. 47. Hutton *op. cit.,* p. 90. Collinson, Rev. J. *History of Somerset,* 1791, 'Keynsham'. See also Poole *op. cit.,* p. 99. Boger tells us that her authority for the story was Butler's, *Lives of the Saints,* 1883.

NEOT : The story is recorded by Boger *op. cit.,* pp. 111-2.

ULRIC : *Ibid,* p. 260. See also Wulfric below.

WIGEFORT : Bett, H. *op. cit.,* p. 52. Other altars, Hutton, *op. cit.,* p. 100.

WULFRIC : See Poole *op. cit.,* pp. 94-8. Tongue, R. L. *op. cit.,* pp. 188-9 has two stories about the saint collected from oral tradition in 1905. The quotations about Wulfric's austerity are taken from Poole *op. cit.,* p. 95.

BLADUD : Boger, E. *op. cit.,* p. 15 provides the genealogy of Bladud as given by Geoffrey of Monmouth. She also records the story of the pigs and the attempted flight, as do Tongue, Poole and Collinson. The Bladud stories, like so many in this chapter, appear to be a mixture of oral tradition, literary allusions and oral tradition perpetuated by literary contact. Warner's *History of Bath* is quoted by Boger *op. cit.,* p. 18.

3 *The Daily Round,* pages 44-58

BUILDING PROCEDURE : Tongue, R. L., Briggs, K. M. (ed.) *Somerset Folklore,* 1965 pp. 16-7.

EXMOOR : Timberscombe, Exmoor, 30.4.71. Collected by R. W. Patten.

CHARMS v WITCHCRAFT : See Mathews, F. W. *Tales of the Blackdown Borderland,* 1923, pp. 105, 106.

HOLED STONE: Mathews, F. W. *op. cit.,* p. 17.

HOLINSHED : Quoted Mathews, *Ibid.*

GLASS BALLS : R. W. Patten, personal communication, 1972.

WHISTLING WOMEN : alternative last line, see C. H. Poole *Customs, Superstitions and Legends of Somerset,* 1877 (2nd ed.), 1970, p. 39.

HENS & COCKS : *Ibid.*

TINGLING EARS : The lore about tingling ears is fairly general, but for antidote see Poole *op. cit.,* p. 42. Cf. shivering when someone walks over your grave.

ITCHING NOSE : O. Knott *Witches of Wessex* (1958), p. 29.

BUTTER PRICE : Collected by R. W. Patten from Horlicks Dairies, Ilminster, 1973.

AMBULANCE OR HEARSE : R. W. Patten, personal communication, 1972.

TEA POT : Ashford, 27.8.72. Collected R. W. Patten. Note that a 'ginger baby' is regarded as a bad thing.

SEE A PIN : O. Knott *op. cit.*, p. 29.

RETURN HOME : See also Smith, A., *Discovering Folklore in Industry*, 1969, p. 9.

SMOKE CATCHER : Seen by the author at Rock Inn, Rock, nr. Taunton. Ruth Tongue told me of the bundle of sticks being used. In the hill villages of Helambu in Nepal smoke from household fires is drawn by large wire baskets of sweet corn husk and straw, there being no other chimney. The ventilation remains totally inadequate.

TATWORTH CANDLE AUCTION : For details of this auction see the article by R. W. Patten in *Folklore*, summer 1970, vol. 81, pp. 132-5.

DATE, TATWORTH CANDLE AUCTION : See Patten, R. W. *Chard and Ilminster News*, 20.4.72.

CHEDZOY CANDLE AUCTION : Patten, R. W. *Folklore*, Spring 1971, vol. 82, pp. 60-1.

CHARD SANDGLASS AUCTION : See Patten, R. W. *Chard and Ilminster News*, 18.11.71.

CONGRESBURY AUCTION : Tongue *op. cit.,* pp. 179-80.

BOGER, E., *Myths, Scenes and Worthies of Somerset, 1887,* pp. 99-100.

STRAPPING AND LUCK MONEY : R. W. Patten, personal communication, 1969.

DRAYTON AND MUCHELNEY SOCIETIES : Collected R. W. Patten, from Drayton, 23.10.72.

LANGPORT CLUB : See Wyatt, I. *The Book of Huish,* 1933, p. 113. Eye-witness account, 26.5.73, R. W. Patten, private communication.

There has since come to my notice a very good general article on Clubs and particularly on the ornamental staff heads in *Somerset Year Book,* 1922, pp. 51ff. called 'Somerset Club Brasses' by E. W. Gun. At the end of the article the editor gives a list of other sources for material on this subject.

BIRD BAITING : Wyatt *op. cit.*, p. 93.

BIRDLORE : Crows, owls, cuckoos, robins and wrens, Poole *op. cit.*, p. 40.

ROBIN'S BREAST : A tradition that obviously postdates Christianity. It would be interesting to know of a non-Christian tradition similar to that found in other cultures where the red breasted bird brings or steals fire (cf. Australian Aborigine).

The alternative version of the robin's breast story was collected from S. Somerset, mid-1950s by R. W. Patten. Ruth Tongue also has a version of the myth where the robin has to fly through the fires of hell (Tongue *op. cit.*, p. 45).

BLACK COCKS : See Tongue *op. cit.*, p. 50. Ruth Tongue's collection of bird lore from the county is most valuable.

HARES : Collected near Ilminster, 1968.

ADDER AND VIPER : Wyatt *op. cit.*, p. 109.

BADGER STREET : Palmer, K. *Oral Folk-tales of Wessex*, pp. 16-7.

WHITE HORSE : Bath, Opie, I. and P *The Lore and Language of Schoolchildren*, 1959, p. 206. The same belief without the qualifying action is also recorded from Bath, but with a prohibition on seeing its tail (Opie *op. cit.*, p. 207).

OAK TREE'S REVENGE : Tongue *op. cit.*, p. 27. Ruth Tongue has a good collection of lore relating to both trees and plants.

BOILMAN : Boger *op. cit.*, p. 589.

ORCHID : Chillington, mid-1950s. Collected R. W. Patten. Cf. the sainfoin (lit. 'healthy hay') which grew at the foot of the cross and so assumed its colour from the same source. See Robin, *supra*. G. H. Browning has this to say about the pimpernel in the book, *Children's Book of Wild Flowers* (1927): 'In Chittlehampton they call the Pimpernel "Urith's Blood" after S. Urith of Chittlehampton was martyred with a sythe and on the same spot where her blood fell the pimpernel grew.' (Quoted from *Wordlore*, No. 1, Feb. 1928, p. 20).

KIDNEY BEANS : West Somerset, 1971. Collected R. W. Patten.

BLACKTHORN : S. Somerset, 1968.

SKYLARKS AND SHEEP : S. Somerset, 1968.

MOON : W. Somerset, 1971. Collected R. W. Patten.

MACKEREL SKY AND NOISY SHEEP : W. Somerset, 1971. Collected R. W. Patten.

RAKE LEFT ON GROUND : Mathews *op. cit.*, p. 14.

4 *Witches and Curses,* pages 59-70

HUISH WITCHCRAFT : Wyatt, I. *The Book of Huish,* 1933, p. 112.

WADEFORD : For the story recorded verbatim, see Palmer, K. *Oral Folktales of Wessex,* 1973, p. 115. The story was collected from Wadeford in 1969.

MOMMET : Wyatt *op. cit.,* p. 112.

PEDLARS : About 20 years ago in Newquay, Cornwall the author heard a gypsy trying to sell clothes pegs to a shop keeper. The shop keeper refused, and the gypsy was heard to say, 'I'll put a curse on 'e if 'e don't buy 'un.'

HOLY WATER : Poole, C. H. *The Customs, Superstitions and Legends of the County of Somerset,* 1877, p. 29.

FROME : *Somerset Year Book,* 1922; C. Somerville Watson, 'Witchcraft in Somerset', pp. 24-25.

ASAFOETIDA : Resinous gum with a strong flavour of garlic.

WITCHCRAFT TEST : *Somerset Year Book,* 1922: C. S. Watson, 'Witchcraft in Somerset', p. 25. Source quoted as, *The Daily Journal,* January 15, 1731, and also *Gentleman's Magazine,* Vol. 1, 1731.

SNAIL TEST : *Wordlore,* Vol. 2, No. 1, Feb. 1927, p. 24.

TOADS : Collected in a personal interview from Ruth Tongue. The informant explained that as a 'Chime Child' she was beyond the power of the witch, so no evil could result from her so closely cuddling the toads. The incident took place at Pitminster.

WITCH'S LADDER : Mathews, F. W. *Tales of the Blackdown Borderland,* 1923, pp. 106-7.

WITCH AND THE DOG : Mathews, *op. cit.,* p. 103.

BRIDGWATER WITCH : Poole *op. cit.,* pp. 56-7. See also Tongue, R. *Somerset Folklore,* 1965, pp. 73-4.

MOTHER LEAKEY : See, Dunton, J. *Athenianism,* 1710, 'The Apparition Evidence'. Scott, Sir W., *Rokeby,* note vii to Canto 2. Hancock, F. *Minehead in the County of Somerset,* 1903, pp. 394-402. Tongue, R. *op. cit.,* p. 84. Hurley, J. *Legends of Exmoor,* 1973, pp. 24-6. Mr Hurley also has Cruickshank's drawing on the cover of his book. It is a tradition that whistling brings sailors bad luck, and to whistle before going to sea will bring on storms.

MOTHER SHIPTON : Hurley *op. cit.,* pp. 21-3.

MADAME JOAN CARNE : Ruth Tongue, personal interview, Crowcombe, 1969. See also Hurley *op. cit.,* pp. 29-31. Tongue *op.*

cit., p. 76, pp. 82-3, p. 107.

NANCY CAMEL : Shepton Mallet local traditions. For literary versions see Tongue *op. cit.*, pp. 83-4; Poole *op. cit.*, pp. 108-9.

MARY ANN BULL : Local tradition, Hinton St George, 1969. Informant, Wool, Dorset, 1971. See also Knott, O. *Witches of Wessex,* 1958, pp. 11-4.

JANE BROOKS : Poole *op. cit.*, pp. 57-60. Glanvil, J. *Saducismus Triumphatus,* 2nd ed., 1688. Translated by Horneck, A., London, 1681.

ELIZABETH STYLE : See also Tongue *op. cit.*, pp. 225-6.

WOOKEY HOLE : Local tradition, Wookey Hole. See also Poole *op. cit.*, p. 130. *Somerset Year Book,* 1905, Vol. iv, p. 193. Tongue *op. cit.*, p. 16. Boger, E. *Myths, Scenes and Worthies of Somerset,* 1887, p. 605.

DRAKE : Traditions collected from Peasmarsh and Crowcombe, 1969. Literary sources are extensive and include; Sydenham, G. F. (ed.), Cameron, A. J. *The History of the Sydenham Family,* 1928, p. 350. *Somerset Year Book,* 1932; C. E. Kille, 'Combe Sydenham', pp. 81-2. Bett, *English Myths and Traditions,* 1952, pp. 48-9. Tongue *op. cit.*, pp. 193-4. Briggs and Tongue *Folktales of England,* 1965, pp. 94-5. Palmer *op. cit.*, pp. 153-4. Hurley *op. cit.*, pp. 10-3. Hurley gives the story in some detail and provides interesting historical material.

5 *Dragons, Giants and Devils,* pages 71-80

CHURCHSTANTON : Mathews, F. W. *Tales of the Blackdown Borderland,* 1923, pp. 73-4.

NAKED BOY : Hurley, J. *Legends of Exmoor,* 1973, pp. 63-4. R. W. Patten, personal communication, 1972. The place is said by local tradition to be the spot where Raleigh dropped dead.

CULM DAVEY : See Ch. 1, p. 29.

STAPLE FITZPAINE : Local tradition, collected 1968.

BROADWAY : Local tradition, collected 1968. See Palmer, K. *Oral Folk-tales of Wessex,* 1973, p. 112.

STANTON DREW : The literature on these traditions is considerable. Perhaps one of the most thorough and best documented source is Grinsell, L. V. *The Folklore of Stanton Drew,* 1973. Anyone interested in a chronological bibliography for the site should read Grinsell. Briefly follow some of the recorded versions of the tradition: Boger, E. *Myths, Scenes and Worthies of Somerset,* 1887, p. 244 (Midsummer's eve). Bett, H. *English Myths and Traditions,* 1952, p. 38 (piper). Hutton, E. *Highways and Byways in Somerset,* 1912, p. 95 (Wood of Bath). Grinsell states that Wood visited Stanton Drew in about 1740, and cites the quotation as Wood, J. *Description of Bath,* 1749, i, p. 148. Grinsell *op. cit.,* p. 7 (Kitty and Johnny). See also Poole, C. H. *The Customs, Superstitions and Legends of the County of Somerset,* 1887, p. 120.

WELLINGTON MONUMENT : Mathews *op. cit.,* p. 94.

WINDWHISTLE : Local tradition, collected from school children, Purtington, 1968. See also, Palmer *op. cit.,* p. 113.

TARR STEPS : Local tradition, but see also Bett, H. *English Legends,* 1952, p. 85. Hutton *op. cit.,* p. 346. Briggs, K. M. and Tongue, R. L. *Folktales of England,* 1965, pp. 105-6. Hurley, J. *op. cit.,* pp. 41-3. Hurley gives this tradition, and several others relevant to Tarr Steps.

ROBIN HOOD'S BUTTS : Mathews *op. cit.,* p. 99.

GIANT'S GRAVE : Local tradition, 1968. See Palmer, K. *op. cit.,* p. 24, Grinsell, L. V. *Proceedings Somerset Archeological and Natural History Society,* Vol. 113, special supplement, p. 1ff.

HAUTVILLE'S QUOIT : Grinsell, L. V. *Folklore of Stanton Drew,* 1973, p. 11. Hutton, E. *op. cit.,* p. 95. Poole *op. cit.,* pp. 117, 119. See also Tongue, R. L. *Somerset Folklore,* 1965, p. 15.

GORME : Local tradition, Bristol, 1956. See Tongue *op. cit.,* pp. 127-8 where Gorme is held responsible for Maes Knoll and the Wansdyke.

QUANTOCKS AND EXMOOR : Briggs and Tongue *op. cit.,* pp. 68-73.

CHURCHSTANTON : Mathews *op. cit.,* p. 97.

BATTLE OF BURFORD : Tatlöck, J. S. P. 'The Dragons of Wessex and Wales', The Mediaeval Academy of America, Massachusetts. An off-print from *Speculum,* Vol. 8, No. 2. April, 1933, p. 223, quoted from *Res Gestae Sax.* 1. 2. (Mon. Germ. Hist. SS 111, 422).

NORTON FITZWARREN : Local tradition, 1968. Rogers, Rev. V. F. E. *The Parish and Church of Norton Fitzwarren,* (Church Guide, 1968). Collinson, Rev. J. *History of Somerset,* 1791, Vol. 3, p. 272. Poole *op. cit.,* p. 103.

SHERVAGE AND KINGSTON ST MARY : Tongue *op. cit.,* pp. 129-31.

ALLER : Boger, E. *op. cit.,* p. 128. Tongue, *op. cit.,* p. 129.

6 *Ghosts and the Grave,* pages 81-91.

JILTED BRIDE : Collected R. W. Patten, Broadway, 12.2.72.

ILMINSTER GIRLS' GRAMMAR SCHOOL : Collected from Broadway, 26.12.71.

HINTON HOUSE : Local tradition, March 1970.

BARDON HOUSE : For a detailed discussion of this location, and the Mary Queen of Scots legend, see Hurley, J. *Legends of Exmoor,* 1973, p. 6ff.

KING ARTHUR : An informant (1968) from Queens Camel told of a woman who came to stay in the town, and was disturbed during the night by strange noises. Next morning she asked the locals if there had been cavalry manoeuvres. She received the reply that the previous night had been 24 June, St John the Baptist's Day. This was when King Arthur and his knights were said to ride the Hunting Causeway to do homage to the Abbot of Glastonbury.

AUBREY : Aubrey's *Brief Lives,* ed. Clark, A. 1898, 2 vols.

POPHAM : The full details of the Littlecote affair are well presented in *Somerset Life,* Vol. 2, No. 7, p. 25.

CATCOTT : See Poole, C. H. *The Customs, Superstitions and Legends of the County of Somerset,* 1877, 2nd ed. 1970, pp. 74-5.

SOUTH PETHERTON : Collected by R. W. Patten, 1.1.71.

HORTON CROSS MOTEL : Collected by R. W. Patten, 23.10.73.

HUISH EPISCOPI : *The Book of Huish,* I. Wyatt, 1933, p. 63.

CHURCHRIGHT : Yeovil school boy, 1973.

BLUE BURCHIES : See also Tongue, R. and Briggs, K. M. (ed.) *Somerset Folklore,* 1965, p. 121.

HOLMAN CLAVEL : Informant, Staple Fitzpaine, 1969.

BLACK DOGS : Ruth Tongue has collected a number which may be studied, *op. cit.,* p. 107. See also Palmer, K. *Oral Folk-tales of Wessex,* 1973, p. 126 ff.

STAPLEY : See also Tongue *op. cit.,* p. 109.

SNELL : F. J. *Book of Exmoor,* 1903. p. 232-4.

ANIMAL GHOSTS : See Palmer *op. cit.,* p. 126 ff.

PAY KNAPP : Mathews, F. W. *Tales of the Blackdown Borderland,* 1923, p. 73. For pigs see Palmer *op. cit.,* p. 47. There is said to be a ghostly red pig in chains under Wood Bridge, near Ashill (local tradition, 14.1.73.)

WOOD COURT : Local tradition, 14.1.73.

MARY HUNT : Local traditions 1972, and informant, Oxenford,

1969. The informant has confused a folklore tradition with a documented murder which took place at Knowle St Giles in 1879.

CANNARD'S GRAVE : Poole *op. cit.*, pp. 109-10. See also Tongue *op. cit.*, pp. 103-4.

JACK WHITE : See Chapter 1, p. 33 and footnote.

WALFORD'S GIBBET : Tongue, R. L. and Briggs, K. M. *Folktales of England,* 1965, pp. 106-7.

NAN BULL : Local tradition, Hinton St George, 1969. See also Palmer *op. cit.*, p. 26.

STOGUMBER : Gallup, N. *Stogumber Church Guide.*

BRAYFORD : Local tradition, Brayford, 3.11.71.

ST DECUMAN'S : Local tradition, 1968. See also Hurley *op. cit.*, p. 14 ff. Poole *op. cit.*, p. 123. Palmer *op. cit.*, pp. 64-5. Briggs and Tongue *op. cit.*, p. 88.

SEAVINGTON ST MICHAEL : Hutton, E. *Highways and Byways in Somerset,* 1912, p. 276.

7 *But Once a Year,* pages 92-108.

CALENDAR CHANGE : The calendar change of 1752 had the following effect. 3 September, 1752 became 14 September 1752. It appears that some people clung tenaciously to the original dates, although they were in fact enumerated by the new system. The pre-1752 date system is generally termed 'Old Style' (O.S.) and the post-1752 system New Style (N.S.). Since festivals were translated back to their old dates, but were called by the New Style, and this process was sometimes not exact, a third category is used here, Folk Style (F.S.).

In practice the result was that – for example – Christmas Day in 1752 was regarded as 14 December (O.S.) and not as a true festival at all. Thus by the time Christmas Day O.S. came along the N.S. calendar had reached 5 Jan. – which was in fact Twelfth Night (N.S.). The next day N.S. 6 January is in fact traditionally regarded as Christmas Day (O.S.) which is an error of one day. The 6 January N.S. equals 26 December O.S. This error is explained by the fact that the twelve days after Christmas had been a holiday period since Roman times, and the Twelfth Day N.S. (6 January N.S.) became easily associated with Christmas Day O.S. Clearly Twelfth Night O.S. should be 5 January O.S. or 16 January N.S. and 17 January has become thought of as Twelfth Night O.S.

BIBLE DIVINATION : Poole, C. H. *The Customs, Superstitions, and Legends of the County of Somerset* (1877, 2nd edn, 1970) pp. 8-9. See also Tongue, R. L. and Briggs, K. M. (ed.) *Somerset Folklore* 1965, pp. 152-3.

PLOUGH SUNDAY : See also Tongue *op. cit.*, p. 153.

HUISH PLOUGHING MATCH : Wyatt, I. *The Book of Huish*, 1933, p. 95.

OLD CHRISTMAS DAY : Informant, Staple Fitzpaine, 1969.

HOLY THORNS : For the holy thorn, and its relationship with Glastonbury, see Chapter 10.

WASSAILING AND THE ASHEN FAGGOT : Palmer, K. and Patten, R. W. 'Some Notes on Wassailing and the Ashen Faggot', *Folklore*, Winter 1971, Vol. 82, pp. 281-91.

VISITING WASSAIL : *Ibid*, R. W. Patten was chiefly responsible for the collection and comparison of the wassailing songs.

APPLE TREE WASSAIL : See also, Walters, C. (ed.) *Bygone Somerset*, 1897, pp. 122-35.

CANDLEMAS : *Wordlore*, Vol. 1, No. 1, Jan.-Feb. 1926, p. 26.

VALENTINES : Opie, I. and P. *The Lore and Language of School Children* (1959, 1967 edn), p. 235.

SHROVE TUESDAY : Local tradition, south Somerset. See also Poole *op. cit.*, p. 10. Opie *op. cit.*, p. 239. Wyatt *op. cit.*, p. 94, *Wordlore*, Vol. 1, No. 1, 1926, p. 27.

EGG SHACKLING : See also Opie *op. cit.*, p. 255, fn. 1.

CLIPPING THE CHURCH : O. E. *clyppan* – to embrace.

STAPLE GROVE : Ruth Tongue, personal communication, 1968.

LANGFORD BUDVILLE : Hutton, E. *Highways and Byways in Somerset*, 1912, p. 235.

LENT COCKING : Cock fights, see Opie *op. cit.*, p. 237, fn. 2. R. L. Tongue, personal communication, 1968. Tongue, R. L. and Briggs, K. M. *op. cit.*, p. 157.

JACK A LENT : *Wordlore*, Vol. 1, No. 1, 1926, p. 26.

HASH MEAT *Ibid.*

CUSSING DAY : See also Tongue and Briggs *op. cit.*, p. 158.

SIMNEL SUNDAY : There follow two recipes for Simnel cake that may be of interest to readers.

1)	6 oz Caster Sugar	1 lb currants
	10 oz flour	4 eggs

2 oz mixed peel   Nutmeg
6 oz butter   1 teasp. baking powder

Beat butter and sugar, add beaten eggs. Mix baking powder and
flour, add. Add fruit and flavouring. Mix well. Half fill a greased
tin lined with grease-proof paper. Add half almond paste. Fill tin
with mixture. Bake 4 hours in slow oven. When cake is half baked
add rest of almond paste, brushing top of cake with egg white
before placing in position.
Almond paste; Add 6 oz ground almonds and $4\frac{1}{2}$ oz caster sugar.
Stir in two egg whites and heat slowly over a low flame until it
forms a paste.
(Mrs. I. Pring, Ilminster, 1974. From a recipe belonging to her
mother, and thought to be over 100 years old.)

2)   1 lb 12 oz butter   2 lb currants
       4 oz fat   2 lb sultanas
       2 lb brown sugar $1\frac{1}{2}$ lb cut mixed peel
       2 pts egg   8 oz ground almonds or hazel nuts
       $2\frac{1}{2}$ lb plain flour $\frac{1}{2}$ oz mixed spice
             Essence of lemon, vanilla and almonds
             Dark colouring.

Cream butter, fat and sugar till light. Add eggs, gradually over 5
minutes. Stir in flour, ground almonds and spice, until clear. Add
fruit and peel.
For a cake of $2\frac{1}{2}$ lb use a 7 inch tin, double-lined with grease-proof
paper. Weigh 1lb cake mixture into tin, and place 8 oz almond paste
on top. Add 1lb cake mix on top, flatten and bake at 350°f. for
about $1\frac{1}{2}$ hours.
When cold brush top with boiled apricot jam and cut out almond
paste to fit top of cake. Remove 5-inch radius from centre, wash
with egg and place in hot oven until 'golden brown' (approx 5
mins.) Brush almond paste with sugar wash (1 oz sugar: 3 oz water)
while still hot. Fill centre with icing and write, 'Simnel' in centre.
N.B. Ground almonds may be creamed with sugar and butter, with
essence and colour.
(Mrs. H. J. Tolley, Ilminster. Tolley's Bakery still make these cakes
from mid Lent until Easter.)

I am grateful to Mrs Pring and Mrs Tolley for the details of these recipes.

PRIMROSE DAY : 'Anniversary of the death (19 April 1881) ... Benjamin Disraeli Earl of Beaconsfield.' (*Oxford English Dict.*) I have not been able to establish that there was an existing folklore festival on this date.

PALM SUNDAY : Tongue and Briggs *op. cit.*, p. 159.

BRENT KNOLL : Collected R. W. Patten, c. 1968.

EASTER SUNDAY : Poole *op. cit.*, p. 11. See also Tongue and Briggs *op. cit.*, pp. 159-60.

MINEHEAD HOBBY HORSE : Patten, R. W. 'Minehead Hobby Horses' *Exmoor Review,* 1973. Poole *op. cit.*, p. 13ff. Ruth Tongue, personal communication, 1968. Informant, Rock, 1966. See also Tongue and Briggs *op. cit.*, pp. 161-2. Savage. J. *History of the Hundred of Carhampton,* (1830). pp. 583-4.

SHEEP SHEARING : Wyatt, I. *op. cit.*, p. 74, p. 75.

SHICK SHACK DAY : *Ibid.*, p. 94.

HARVEST STOOK : Informant, Crowcombe, 1968.

CORN DOLLY : *Ibid.*

TATWORTH : Informant, 1932.

EAST BRENT : 'West County Customs', *English Dance and Song,* Spring 1971.

MICHAELMAS : Poole *op. cit.*, p. 23, quoting from Brand's *Observation on Popular Antiquities,* 2 Vols, 1813.

HALLOWE'EN : Hallowe'en was the New Year's Eve of the Celtic Calendar. See Palmer, K. *Oral Folktales of Wessex,* 1973, pp. 58-9.

BRENDON HILLS : Brendon Hills, local tradition, 1968. See also Tongue and Briggs *op. cit.*, pp. 170-1.

PUNKIES : Palmer, K. 'Punkies', *Folklore,* Vol 83, Autumn 1972. pp. 240-4. Palmer, K. *Oral Folk-tales of Wessex,* 1973, pp. 84-8. *Chard and Ilminster News,* November 1973.

HORTON : Patten, R. W. personal communication. He also supplied the information about Drayton and Donyatt and the 1972 Lopen Punkie Night.

8 *An Apple a Day,* pages 109-115

HALF AN ONION : Lopen, 1973, collected R. W. Patten.

COMMUNION WINE : Tatworth, 1932.

WARTS : *Additional*: Horton, 1973. Collected R. W. Patten.

Charmer: Broadway, 1967. Purchase: Ilminster, 1965. Bean pod; Drayton & Langport, 1972. Collected by R. W. Patten. Eldershoot: Poole, C. H. *Customs, Superstitions and Legends of the County of Somerset*, 2nd ed., 1970, p. 52.Cows: Cudworth, 1950. Collected R. W. Patten.

BOILS : Personal communication, R. W. Patten, 1973.

SORES : Cudworth, 1955. Collected R. W. Patten.

CARBUNCLES : Timberscombe, 1971.

FLICK : 'Fleck, Obs. exc. dial, also flick = flare. 1881, *I of Wight Gloss*, Flick or Vlick. The lard of the inside of a pig. 1883. *Hampsh Gloss*; Fleck, the fat of a pig before it is boiled down into lard.' *Oxford English Dictionary.*

TOOTHACHE : Mathews, F. W. *Tales of the Blackdown Borderland*, 1923, p. 15.

COLDS : Tea, lopen, 1973. Collected R. W. Patten.

EYES : Hurley, J. *Legends of Exmoor*, 1973, p. 3.

SORE THROAT : Dirty sock, Broadway, collected R. W. Patten.

COUGHS : Poole *op. cit.*, p. 52.

QUINSY : Knott, O. *Witches of Wessex*, 1958, p. 42. Also weak backs.

AGUE : Poole *op. cit.*, p. 52.

PILES : Name changed to avoid embarrassment. Personal collection, 1970.

HERNIA : Huish, Wyatt, I. *The Book of Huish*, 1933, p. 112. Mathews *op. cit.*, p. 15.

KING'S EVIL : *Oxford English Dictionary*. Monmouth: Boger, E. *Myths, Scenes and Worthies of Somerset*, 1887, p. 580.

CHARLES II : *Ibid.*

WHOOPING COUGH : Mathews *op. cit.*, p. 15.

RHEUMATISM : Stinging nettles, south Somerset, collected R. W. Patten.

9 *Illicit Gains*, pages 116-123

SHEPTON GAOL : *Wordlore*, Vol. 1, No. 1, 1926, p. 36.

PROFANE OATHS : *Wordlore, op. cit.*, p. 56. See also Opie, I. and P. *Lore and Language of School Children* (1959. 1967 edn), p. 121 ff. Of particular importance is the footnote to page 122.

PIE LANE : Bristol. *Wordlore,* Vol. 1, No. 3, 1926, p. 206.

CULMSTOCK : Mathews, F. W. *Tales of the Blackdown Borderland,* 1923, p. 30.

SHEEP-STEALING : Mathews *op. cit.,* p. 109. Tongue, R. L. and Briggs, K. M. (ed.) *Somerset Folklore,* 1965, p. 49. Ruth Tongue's versions are more detailed and show some small variation. See also Briggs, K. M. *Dictionary of British Folktales,* 1970. Part A, Vol. 11. 'Farmer Tickle and the Owl', p. 83. Palmer, K. *Oral Folktales of Wessex,* 1973, pp. 29-30.

PENAL CODE : 'There were 220 offences for which the death penalty could be imposed ... it was 1832 before housebreaking, sheep-stealing and forgery ceased to be on the list, but after 1838 no one was hanged except for murder or attempted murder.' Thomson, D. *England in the 19th Century* (1950, 1964 edn) pp. 16-17.

FAGGUS : Hurley, J. *Legends of Exmoor,* 1973 p. 58 f. Full details of the Faggus legend are described by Hurley, and anyone interested in following the legend should consult Hurley's collection of stories and references about the highwayman.

WINDWHISTLE : Oral traditions, 1968-9. For other traditions see Palmer *op. cit.,* p. 30 ff.

POCOCK : Collected from Ruth Tongue, Crowcombe, 1968.

TURPIN : See also Palmer *op. cit.,* p. 33.

SMUGGLING : See Trail, H. D. *Social England,* 1894, Vol. 11, p. 350.

Routes; Rattenbury, J. *Memoirs of a Smuggler,* 1837. p. 1 ff. Blackdowns; Mathews *op. cit.,* pp. 42-54.

Mathews has a detailed collection of stories from the area.

BRANDY BRIDGE : Informant, Bickenhall, 1969.

HINTON ST GEORGE : Oral traditions, 1969. See also Palmer *op. cit.,* p. 167.

WINDWHISTLE : Tongue *op. cit.,* pp. 96-7. Munford, *Ghosts and Legends of South Somerset* (London, 1922) pp. 20-30. Local tradition collected from Windwhistle, 1969.

10 *History as They Saw it,* pages 124-137

ARTHUR : See Palmer, K. *Oral Folk-tales of Wessex,* 1973, pp. 155-6. Susan M. Pearce, 'The Cornish Elements in the Arthurian Tradition', in *Folklore,* Vol. 85, Autumn 1974, pp. 145-163, discusses the false etymology that links Arthur with Glastonbury.

HOLY THORN : Literary references are considerable. Traditions discussed are in general circulation. See also Camden, W. *A Chorographical Description of Great Britain and Ireland* (Revised and translated from the Latin, 1722) E. Gibbon, 2nd ed. Vol. 1, p. 79. Collinson, J. *History of Somerset,* Bath 1791, 3 vols, Vol. 2, p. 265. Poole, C. H. *Customs, Superstitions and Legends of the County of Somerset,* 1877, 2nd ed., 1970, p. 84. Bett, H. *English Myths and Traditions,* 1952, p. 56. Hutton, E. *Highways and Byways in Somerset,* 1912, pp. 168-9. Boger, E. *Myths, Scenes and Worthies of Somerset,* 1887, p. 32. J. Hurley in his *Legends of Exmoor,* 1973, pp. 46-7 tells that Christ visited Glenthorne with Joseph and there founded a spring of water that never fails.

WALNUT : Hutton *op. cit.,* p. 169.

THORN : *Ibid.,* p. 165.

CHALICE HILL : *Ibid.,* p. 168.

BETT H : *English Legends,* 1952, p. 1 ff. Hutton *op. cit.,* p. 161 tells that the excavation was witnessed by Adam de Domerham, and describes it accordingly. See also Boger *op. cit.,* pp. 58-9.

CAMELOT : See Chapter 1, p. 26.

ALFRED : Poole *op. cit.,* pp. 65-8. Boger *op. cit.,* pp. 117-8. For another Alfred legend see Tongue, R. L. *Somerset Folklore,* ed. K. M. Briggs, 1965, p. 191.

MUCHELNEY : See Collinson *op. cit.,* Vol. 3, p. 134. Boger *op. cit.,* p. 183. Hutton tells us that the Abbey was founded after the Battle of Brunanburgh. See also Palmer *op. cit.,* p. 53.

MONTECUTE : Hutton *op. cit.,* pp. 249-51. Boger *op. cit.,* p. 210.

BECKET : Hurley *op. cit.,* pp. 45-6.

WOLSEY : Oral traditions collected Hinton St George and Lopen, 1969. See also Street, J. *The Mynster of the Ile,* Ilminster and Taunton, 1904, p. 67. Boger *op. cit.,* p. 418.

HULBERT : *Proceedings of the Somerset Archeological and Natural History Society,* Vol. 82, 1936, pp. 127-8.

DUNSTER : Snell, F. J. *A Book of Exmoor,* 1903, p. 23. Fuller; see Boger *op. cit.,* p. 335.

HUISH : Wyatt, I. *The Book of Huish,* 1933, p. 43.

CATCOTT : Poole *op. cit.,* pp. 74-5.

NORTON ST PHILIP : Hutton *op. cit.,* p. 78.

WHITELACKINGTON : For a full account of Monmouth's visit to the place see Palmer *op. cit.*, pp. 160-1.

ALFORD : Poole *op. cit.*, p. 106.

RHINE : Bett, H. *English Myths and Traditions*, 1952, p. 81.

STREET : Briggs K. M. and Tongue, R. L. *Folktales of England*, 1965, p. 96.

CHURCHILL : See Palmer, *op. cit.*, pp. 54-7.

11 *Entertainment and Humour*, pages 138-150

FIVES : *Oxford English Dictionary*, Reference to Buckland; Mathews, F. W. *Tales of the Blackdown Borderland*, 1923, p. 34. *Journal of English Dance and Song*, Autumn, 1973. Correspondence.

List of fives walls and adaptations in Somerset.

Bishops Lydeard; behind the *Lethbridge Arms* Inn.

Hinton St George; behind the *Poulett Arms.*

Ilminster; now destroyed.

Shepton Beauchamp; behind the *New Inn.*

South Petherton; behind the *Crown Inn.*

Stoke under Ham; behind the *Fleur de Lis.*

Adaptations;

Curry Rivel; end of cottage walls.

Martock; church tower.

Montecute; church tower.

West Buckland; church tower.

MUMMERS : North Somerset, see *Somerset Year Book,* 1931, Whittaker, O. H. 'The Mummers', p. 39 ff. Tongue, R. L. *Somerset Folklore,* ed. K. M. Briggs, 1965, p. 174. Poole, *Customs, Superstitions and Legends of the County of Somerset,* 1877, 1970 ed. p. 5.

DRAYTON : 'Jan', collected by R. W. Patten, 25.7.71 from C. Showers, Drayton. Mr Showers learnt the story 50 years previously from Fred Spearing. 'Sheepshead Stew'; *Ibid.*, from Mr Showers' personal collection of songs and stories.

ROLLS-ROYCE : See also Sanderson S. F. 'The Folklore of the Motor Car', *Folklore,* Vol. 80 1969 pp. 241-222.

DRAYTON : 'The Cat', C. Showers, 6.2.71. Collected by R. W. Patten.

TWO CATS : Collected by R. W. Patten. See also Opie, I. and P. *The Lore and Language of School Children,* 1959, 1967 ed. p. 23 for similar version from Portsmouth, and several others.

JACOB STONE : Mathews, *op. cit.*, p. 109. See also, Palmer, K. *Oral Folk-tales of Wessex,* 1973, p. 40.

PLACE RHYMES : Frome: *Wordlore,* Vol. 1, No. 4, August 1926, p. 152.

Devil: South Somerset, 1969.

Oare: *Wordlore, op. cit.*, and Hurley, J. *Legends of Exmoor,* 1973, p. 52.

Muchelney: Muchelney 1973, collected R. W. Patten. See also Tongue *op. cit.*, p. 214. Palmer *op. cit.*, p. 20.

RIDDLES : Farmer and dressmaker; Merriott, January, 1973, collected R. W. Patten.

Umbrella; *Ibid.*, Andrew; *Ibid.*

Husband and wife; Bristol, 1950s. Recently a story was told illustrating the unequal position women have in society; 'A man goes for a drive with his son, and they are involved in an accident. The father is killed, the son taken to hospital for an emergency operation. The surgeon is called for the operation, but seeing the boy says; "I can't operate on this boy, he is my son". How do you account for this?

Tuft on palm of hand; Wyatt, I. *The Book of Huish,* 1933, p. 112.

Madness: very general.

NONSENSE : 'What's the time', Chillington School, 1950s. Collected R. W. Patten, See also Opie *op. cit.*, p. 44.

'Behave yourself nicely', Horton, 1970. Collected R. W. Patten.

'Spider, spider', Broadway 1972. Collected R. W. Patten.

'Ask no questions', 1950, Bristol. Also reported from Chillington 1950s in contracted form.

'I took myself to the pictures,' north Somerset, 1950s. Also reported from south Somerset, 1970. See Opie, *op. cit.*, p. 25. The rhyme is obviously very general. 'One fine day', Opie, *loc. cit.* Versions quoted here from personal memory, south Somerset, 1960.

WORK SONGS : 'Broad and Beauty', Mathews, *op. cit.*, p. 21. 'He, hi, ho', *Ibid.*

TOASTS : 'Now I've travelled all day'. Drayton, 1973, Collected R. W. Patten.

'Good luck', *Somerset Year Book,* 1922, p. 32.

'Here's Health', *Ibid.*

'I like to zee 'ee come', *Ibid,* collected from the North Petherton area.

DRINKING : 'Aw, he'em like a hedgehog', Mathews *op. cit.*, p. 20.
'Tanglefoot', East Coker, July, 1973. Collected R. W. Patten.
'Beer on Cider'. Personal collection. See also Wyatt, I. *The Book of Huish,* 1933, p. 112 who gives the rhyme the other way about. Try it and see!
'Let the wealthy and the great', D. N. Coleman, B. A. thesis (Unpublished) Leeds University, 'Cider making in North and Central Somerset'.
'He that by the plough must thrive', *Ibid.*
'De Spise me not', *Wordlore,* Vol. 2, No. 2, April 1927, p. 49.

Somerset Folklife Museums

This list includes only those collections of interest to the folklorist.

Somerset County Museum, Taunton Castle, Taunton.

Weston-Super-Mare Museum and Art Gallery, The Boulevard, Weston-Super-Mare.

The Somerset Rural Life Museum, Abbey Barn, Glastonbury is due to open in 1976.

Dowlish Wake, near Ilminster, has a fascinating collection housed in an old barn. Perry Bros., Cider Manufacturers, Dowlish Wake.

Bibliography

BOOKS LISTED here are sources for Somerset folklore. Works referred to only a few times are not included, and details of these will be found in the notes as appropriate.

The place of publication is London, unless otherwise stated.

BETT, H. *English Legends* (London, New York, Toronto, Sydney, 1950, reprinted 1952).
   English Myths and Traditions (London, New York, Toronto, Sydney 1952).

BOGER, E. *Myths, Scenes and Worthies of Somerset* (1887)

BOVET, R. *Pandaemonium or the Devil's Cloyster* (1684)

CAMDEN, W. A. *Chorographical Description of Great Britain and Ireland* (Revised and translated from the Latin, 1722, E. Gibson. 2 vols, 2nd edn)

COLLINSON, REV. J. *History of Somerset,* 3 vols with index, (Bath, 1791)

GRAY, H. St George, 'Whitelackington and the Duke of Monmouth', reprinted from *Proceedings of Somerset Archeological Society,* Vol. LXXIII (1927)

GRESWELL, W. H. P. *The Forest and Deer Parks of Somerset* (1905)

HORNE, DOM E. *Somerset Holy Wells* (Somerset Folk Press, 1923)

HORTSMAN, ED. Translation of the Life of S Decuman, as printed in *Nova Legenda Anglie,* Wynkyn de Warde (1516, Vol. 1; Oxford 1901)

HURLEY, J. *Legends of Exmoor* (Dalverton, 1973)

HUTTON, E. *Highways and Byways in Somerset* (1912)

KNIGHT, F. A. *Sea-board of Mendips* (1915) *Heart of Mendip* (1902)

LACKINGTON, J. *Life of Lackington* 13th edn, (1793)

MATHEWS, F. W. *Tales of the Blackdown Borderland* (Somerset Folk Press, 1923)

MUNFORD, G. F. *Ghosts and Legends of South Somerset* (Somerset Folk Press, 1922, 2nd edn 1922)
   The Somerset Folk Scene (1922)

OPIE, I. and P. *The Lore and Language of School Children* (1959, 1967, edn.)

PAGE, W. (ed.) *Victoria History of Somerset,* 2 vols (1906)

PALMER, K. 'Some Notes on Wassailing and the Ashen Faggot', *Folklore,* Winter 1971, Vol. 82. pp. 281-91 (with R. W. Patten)

'Punkies', *Folklore,* 1972. Vol. 83. pp. 240-4.

Oral Folk-tales of Wessex, (Newton Abbot, 1973).

PATTEN, R. W. 'Tatworth Candle Auction', *Folklore,* Summer 1970, Vol. 81, pp. 132-5.

'Chedzoy Candle Auction, *Folklore,* Spring 1971, Vol. 82, pp. 60-81

(with K. Palmer). 'Some Notes on Wassailing and the Ashen Faggot', *Folklore,* Winter 1971, Vol. 82, pp. 281-91.

Exmoor Custom and Song (Dulverton, 1974)

POOLE, C. H. *The Customs, Superstitions and Legends of the County of Somerset* (1877, 2nd edn, Guernsey, 1970)

Proceedings of the Somerset Archaeological and Natural History Society, published annually since 1849, Taunton, Index Vol. 1-20 (1876)

PULMAN, G. P. R. *The Book of the Axe* (1854)

RADFORD, W. L. 'A Manorial History of Donyatt', reprinted from *Somerset County Herald*

SHILLIBEAR, H. B. *Ancient Customs of the Manor of Taunton Deane* (1821)

SIXSMITH, R. A. *Staple Fitzpaine and the Forest of Neroche* (Taunton, 1958)

SNELL, F. J. Book of Exmoor (1903)

Somerset Year Book 1905-1939

TONGUE, R. L. *Forgotten Folktales of the English Counties* (1970)

TONGUE, R. L., and BRIGGS, K. M. (ed) *Somerset Folklore* (1965) *Folktales of England* (1965)

TREHARNE, R. F. *The Glastonbury Legends* (1967)

WALTERS, C. (ed.) *Bygone Somerset* (1897)

'Calendar of Customs, Superstitions, Weather Lore, of the County of Somerset', reprinted from the *Somerset County Herald* (1920)

WHISTLER, C. W. *Quantock Folklore* (1907)

Wordlore, 1926-1928, Vols 1-3

WYATT, I. *The Book of Huish* (Yeovil, 1933)

Index of Tale Types

Numbers with no letter prefix are from Antti Aarne and Stith Thompson, *The Types of the Folktale*, (1961). ML prefix indicates number from R.Th. Christiansen, *The Migratory Legends*, (1958).

Motif Index

These numbers are from Stith Thompson, *Motif Index of Folk Literature*, 1966.

General Index